JEAN-LOUIS FORAIN

THE IMPRESSIONIST YEARS

The publication of this catalogue

is made possible

through the generosity

of

The Hugo Dixon Foundation

JEAN-LOUIS FORAIN

THE IMPRESSIONIST YEARS
THE DIXON GALLERY AND GARDENS COLLECTION

THEODORE REFF

FLORENCE VALDÈS-FORAIN

WITH INTRODUCTORY ESSAY BY
JOHN E. BUCHANAN, JR.

ORGANIZED AND CIRCULATED BY THE DIXON GALLERY AND GARDENS, MEMPHIS, TENNESSEE

Exhibition Venues

Van Gogh Museum
Amsterdam, Netherlands
March 10 - May 14, 1995

Fondation de L'Hermitage
Lausanne, Switzerland
October 19, 1995 - January 7, 1996

The Burrell Collection
Glasgow, Scotland
June 16 - September 3, 1995

Galerie Hopkins-Thomas
Paris, France
March 15 - May 15, 1996

Library of Congress Cataloging-in-Publication Data
Dixon Gallery and Gardens.
 Jean-Louis Forain : the Impressionist years : the Dixon Gallery
and Gardens Collection / Theodore Reff, Florence Valdès-Forain :
with introductory essay by John E. Buchanan, Jr.
  p. cm.
  Exhibition catalog.
  ISBN 0-945064-00-4
  1. Forain, Jean Louis, 1852-1931--Exhibitions. 2. Impressioism
(Art)--France--Exhibitions. 3. Art--Tennessee--Memphis-
-Exhibitions. 4. Dixon Gallery and Gardens--Exhibitions. I. Reff,
Theodore. II. Valdès-Forain, Florence, 1961- III. Title.
N6853.F6A4 1995   95-6905
760'.092--dc20   CIP

Editor: Liz Conway
Design: Kay Robinson
Technical Editors: Sheila K. Tabakoff, Neville Gay, Shannon Kennedy, Yolande Welch
Printing and Color Separations: Lithograph Printing Company
Paper: International Paper Company
Binding: Universal Bookbindery, Inc.

Forain Collection Photography: Pete Ceren - cat. nos. 4, 6, 9, 11, 12, 17, 19, 24, 25, 36, 37, 43, 47, 48, 49, 50, 51, 55.
Remaining Forain Collection photography courtesy of Galerie Hopkins-Thomas, Paris.

Collateral Photographs courtesy of: The Art Institute of Chicago, Chicago; Bibliotheque Nationale, Paris; Boston Public Library, Boston; The British Museum, London; Sterling and Francine Clark Art Institute, Williamstown, Massachusetts; The Dixon Gallery and Gardens, Memphis; The Fogg Art Museum, Harvard University Art Museums, Cambridge, Massachusetts; Richard Green, London; The Guardsmark, Inc. Collection, Memphis; M. and Mme. Maréchaux, Paris; The Metropolitan Museum of Art, New York; Musée de la Ville, Paris; Musée du Louvre, Paris; Musée d'Orsay, Paris; Musée du Petit Palais, Paris; Museum of Fine Arts, Springfield, Massachusetts; National Gallery of Art, Washington, D.C.; The Walters Art Gallery, Baltimore. The photographs are copyrighted by the lending institutions with all rights reserved.

Photographs of Jean-Louis Forain and his familiy as well as collateral photographs for fig. nos. 10, 14, 19-22, 25, 26, 31 courtesy of the Forain Family Archives.

The chronology of Jean-Louis Forain's life, written by Janine Chagnaud-Forain is reprinted with permission from *Jean-Louis Forain: Artist, Realist, Humanist*, International Exhibitions Foundation, Washington, D.C., 1982-1983.

Cover
Jean-Louis Forain. *Woman with a Fan,* c. 1883. Museum purchase, partially supported by Mrs. James D. Robinson, Mrs. John Sneed Williams, and the estate of Louise Richardson Dodd, The Dixon Gallery and Gardens, Memphis. Cat. no. 17.

CONTENTS

ACKNOWLEDGMENTS

The acquisition of the Forain Collection and its subsequent international tour has been an adventure of connoisseurship, scholarship and excitement for all those involved in the process. The decision for The Dixon Gallery and Gardens to acquire the Forain Collection was a natural one. The Dixon's primary mission to to collect and exhibit works by the French Impressionists who showed at one of the eight group Impressionist exhibitions which took place between 1874 and 1886.

From the very beginning, former Dixon Director John E. Buchanan, Jr. has played a pivotal role. He discovered the Collection, initiated extensive research on it, and then sought the funds to acquire it for the Dixon.

The acquisition iself was made possible through the immediate and generous response of Mr. and Mrs. J. Lester Crain, Mr. and Mrs. J.R. Hyde, III, Mr. and Mrs. Joseph Orgill, III, and Mr. and Mrs. Michael D. Rose. Their on-going support of the Dixon and its major projects has been and continues to be vital.

With interest in the Dixon's Forain Collection at an all time high, the decision was made to mount an international tour of the works. Beginning in Amsterdam, the Forain Collection will tour Europe before returning to its Memphis home at The Dixon Gallery and Gardens. After allowing the works "to rest," a major United States tour will commence.

We are grateful to the high degree of scholarship associated with this project. Ground-breaking new information regarding Forain and his participation in the original Impressionist exhibitions is presented in this catalogue. The dedicated efforts of Dr. Theodore Reff, professor of art history at Columbia University, and Mme. Florence Valdès-Forain, the artist's great grand-daughter and a doctoral candidate in art history at the Sorbonne, made these finds possible.

We sincerely appreciate the support and professionalism exhibited by the personnel at the various venues: Dr. Ronald de Leeuw, Director, and Andreas Blühm, Head of Exhibitions, Van Gogh Museum; Julian Spalding, Director, and Stefan van Raay, Senior Curator of Art, Glasgow Museums, and Vivien Hamilton, Curator, The Burrell Collection; François Daulte, Director, Fondation de l'Hermitage; and Waring Hopkins, Owner, Galerie Hopkins-Thomas.

The commitment of Herbert "Dutch" Akers and the Lithograph Printing Company team have helped make this exhibition catalogue possible. We are grateful for their involvement as well as the technical excellence and outstanding color reproduction always associated with their firm. The Coated Publication and Bristols Groups of International Paper and Zanders USA, a division of International Paper, generously assisted with this catalogue. Universal Bookbindery Inc, San Antonio, also contributed to the catalogue project.

We sincerely appreciate the meticulous attention to detail evidenced by the capable professionals involved with the exhibition tour. Conservator Martina Yamin prepared the works for their international tour. Arie de Vries and Jim Conboy of Creative Crating, Inc. handled crating and packing. David Epstein of Masterpiece International, Inc. supervised shipping and customs clearances.

Throughout the acquisition, exhibition development, and catalogue production process, the Dixon staff has, as always, performed beyond all expectations. The keen eyes and uncompromising standards of Curator of Collections Sheila K. Tabakoff and her curatorial staff, Shannon Kennedy, Marilyn Rhea, Deborah Bass and Lisa Incardona, have ensured scholarly integrity to all aspects of the project. Administrative

Assistant Sally Kee helped to coordinate the needs and activities of all project principals, and her assistance was invaluable. Other Dixon staff members who contributed to the success of this project include Suzy Carpenter, Jane Faquin, Neville Gay, Charles Robinson, James Starks, and Robert Jones.

Serving as an adjunct to the Dixon staff was catalogue editor and production supervisor Liz Conway.   She guided the creative team which included Forain Collection photographer Pete Ceren and Kay Robinson, the catalogue's graphic designer. Their combined talents and perseverance ensured a timely completion of the catalogue.

On behalf of catalogue author Florence Valdès-Forain we extend a special thank you to her mother, Mrs. Janine Chagnaud-Forain, granddaughter of Jean-Louis Forain, for her help in documentation, research and photograph acquisition. Mme. Valdès-Forain also wishes to thank Dr. Theodore Reff for his valuable advice; and to extend appreciation to Ambassador and Mrs. Donald Norland; Professor and Mrs. Daniel Delakas; Mme. Marie-Caroline van Herpen, Garlerie Hopkins-Thomas; Mme. Kate Carot; M. and Mme. Eric Peyrard; M. and Mme. Phillippe Maréchaux; and Mr. Antoine Salomon.

In closing, the Board of Trustees of The Dixon Gallery and Gardens under the dynamic leadership of S. Herbert Rhea continues its remarkable tradition of involvement by giving this project their total support. Their commitment to excellence and active participation has enabled the Dixon staff to successfully tackle a project of this magnitude.

Katherine C. Lawrence
Acting Director

Jean-Louis Forain: The Dixon Collection

by John E. Buchanan, Jr.

This publication documents the Dixon's collection of Impressionist works by the late nineteenth century French artist, Jean-Louis Forain. Through the study of this body of work, it is our intention to illumine Forain's involvement in the Impressionist movement (especially his relationship with Degas), investigate his obsession with dancers as well as the worlds of high and low society of the *belle epoque,* and amplify the unique voice of this artist who as a powerful social commentator and artistic force cut a broad swath through late nineteenth century Paris.

Comprised of 58 works including drawings, watercolors, paintings and etchings executed during Forain's early years as an artist, the collection was assembled almost entirely by the Galerie Hopkins-Thomas, Paris, whose acquaintance I made in the fall of 1992. From that time forward until its purchase in 1993, it became evident that with this single acquisition The Dixon Gallery and Gardens could establish itself as a major international repository for Forain's work and thereby underscore its uniqueness of specializing in works of French Impressionism. The collection put together by Waring Hopkins over approximately a decade would join the Dixon's earlier purchase made in 1987 of *Woman with a Fan* (cat. no. 17) by Forain.

Although examined generally over the past century, most notably by Lillian Browse and most recently by Alicia Faxon on his print making, Forain's Impressionist works have received relatively cursory attention. Best known for his journalist drawings and prints done in a sneering Parisian vein, Forain also participated in the Impressionist movement for a quarter of a century, roughly up until 1900. During this time, he produced the occasional masterpiece with a flavor entirely of its own, many

of which are worthy of the same admiration received by his more frequently and critically reviewed graphic works.

The pictures by Forain in the Dixon's collection also provide numerous visual references to those of his contemporaries, especially Manet, Degas, Cassatt and Renoir. In general, their art shares a common interest in light, a free painterly brush stroke, scenes *en plein air* and in particular a realist subject matter. Forain, however, captures in his uniquely serio-comic fashion *la vie moderne* – the worlds of the café, brothel, and race track – as well as the "elegant woman" and the ballet dancer, both on and off stage.

Forain showed in four of the eight group Impressionist exhibitions held between 1874 and 1886. At the time of the major acquisition from the Galerie Hopkins-Thomas, it was known that at least three of the Dixon's pictures figured in these exhibitions: *At the Café* (cat. no. 7), *The Client* (cat. no. 1) and *Woman with a Fan.* This acquisition would thereby advance another of the Dixon's priorities to collect works that had been featured in one of the group exhibitions. Better still, through the subsequent research of Dr. Theodore Reff and the artist's great-grand daughter, Florence Valdès-Forain, this list today can be expanded to include *The Debutante* (cat. no. 20) and *On the Verses of Verlaine, a Rogue Takes a Stroll in the Country* (cat. no. 43).

In addition, through a closer examination, the pastel previously known as *Chez la modiste* and believed historically to be by Forain is now retitled *La Dernière touche* and re-attributed to Forain's contemporary Paul Helleu. This turn of events is not at all a disappointment, only a surprise to past owners, the dealers through whom the work passed, scholars who published it as Forain and even the Forain family who knew it and did not question its authenticity.

Paul César Helleu. *La Dernièr touche*, c. 1885. Pastel on paper. The Dixon Gallery and Gardens, Memphis, Tennessee.

Only with my discovery of what appears to be the name "Helleu" faintly inscribed and almost invisible in normal light near the upper left corner of the work, did suspicion about the pastel's authorship arise. Following a complete technical examination by conservator Martina Yamin, the name was validated as Helleu's signature. Dixon Curator of Collections Sheila K. Tabakoff contacted Helleu's daughter, Madame Howard-Johnston, the recognized expert on his work, who revealed that she owns a watercolor by Helleu showing the same still life with a bowler hat and cane that appears in *La Dernière touche*. Such a cane, by the way, had been given to Helleu by John Singer Sargent, recounts Madame Howard-Johnston, who also remembers speaking with Forain, himself, regarding his admiration of Helleu's work. Armed with this information, Dr. Reff conducted an in-depth study for proper attribution of the pastel and has concluded that it was executed by Helleu and not Forain.

About the Artist

Although Forain was full of observations about the world in which he lived and freely commented on the lives of others, he was reticent to provide many revelations about his own life. The facts about his evolution as an artist are few and fairly straightforward. I report them here to set up the two essays which follow.

Jean-Louis Forain was born in Reims, France, on October 23, 1852. After moving to Paris in 1860, Forain began his study of art by sketching at the Louvre. He then spent a brief period at the *Ecole des Beaux-Arts* in the *atelier* of Jean-Léon Gérôme, before studying under the painter André Gill and the sculptor Jean-Baptiste Carpeaux.

After participating in the Franco-Prussian War, Forain returned to Paris where he met and befriended poets Paul Verlaine and Arthur Rimbaud. In the early 1870s, he also became a member of an artistic circle which met at the Café de la Nouvelle-Athénes and which included among its members Anatole France, Edouard Manet, Edgar Degas, and the art critic J.–K. Huysmans. Degas became a life-long friend of Forain and an important influence on his art. It was he who urged Forain to join the fourth exhibition of Independent Artists in 1879.

Although the subjects of the theater and the world of the dancer are ones which Forain shared with Degas, Forain's reputation has lived far too long in the shadow of his mentor. We have called upon Dr. Reff to address Forain's rightful place in the Impressionist movement and his true relationship to Degas and his other contemporaries. In his essay which follows entitled, "Le Petit Forain and Monsieur Degas," Dr. Reff clearly establishes not only the mutual influence of one artist on the other but also their distinct and differing approaches to the dance and the dancer.

Forain eventually met with great commercial success. He exhibited at the Salon in 1884 and 1885, and in 1893 he was awarded the *Chevalier de la Légion d'Honneur.*

His satirical drawings were published in *Le Courrier* and *Le Figaro*. Forain is considered by many scholars to be the greatest political and social satirist since Goya and Daumier.

In 1900, Forain's style underwent a change, both in terms of technique and subject matter. He turned away from the colorful palette and style of his Impressionist works to a more somber portrayal of religious subjects and the workings of the French legal system which dominated his art for the remainder of his career. He died in 1931.

In her essay "A Portrait of Jean-Louis Forain" which is included in this volume, Florence Valdès-Forain, provides further insight into the artist's biography and especially into his personality as only the closest family accounts and memories can offer. In particular, anecdotal information on Forain's later life following his marriage to Jeanne Bosc in 1891 is made known to us by Florence through her mother Janine, who was raised by the latter's grandmother, Jeanne Bosc-Forain.

Acknowledgements

There are a number of individuals who have contributed to this artistic discovery and re-examination of the Impressionist work of Jean-Louis Forain. Waring Hopkins had the foresight and knowledge to collect this period of the artist's work at a time when it was out of step with the trends of art history and the art market. The Dixon's decision to move forward on this rather daring opportunity to create a Forain collection virtually overnight was validated by experts: Dr. Richard R. Brettell, Dr. Alicia Faxon, Dr. Charles A. Moffett, Dr. Theodore Reff and Dr. Paul Tucker. Martha Parrish also provided insights in advance of the acquisition and, in fact, was the source for the Dixon's original interest in the artist and its initial acquisition of *Woman with a Fan*.

Input from consultants Barbara Divver, New York, and Florence Herrenschmidt, Paris, also aided the process.

In addition to her scholarly contributions to the catalogue, recognition and appreciation are due to Florence Valdès-Forain for her encouragement and that of her parents Monsieur and Madame Jean Chagnaud-Forain. Janine Chagnaud-Forain, author of Forain's *catalogue raisonné*, embraces the idea of the Dixon's establishment of a Forain study center.

Dixon Acting Director Katherine Lawrence has guided the international exhibition tour and its accompanying catalogue projects with grace, determination and profound respect for all parties involved.

And, finally, the idea to enhance the Dixon's permanent collection with this cache of Forains was only made possible through the generosity of the museum's close patrons: Lester and Brenda Crain, Pitt and Barbara Hyde, Joe and Irene Orgill, and Mike and Gayle Rose. Herbert Rhea, Chairman of the museum's Board of Trustees, deserves special commendation for his bold and visionary leadership in making this project a reality.

Le Petit Forain and Monsieur Degas

by Theodore Reff

At the beginning of his career, the years from 1875 to 1895, when Forain produced the majority of the works in this exhibition, the older artist who most influenced his choices among modern subjects and his modes of seeing and treating them, and the one who also shaped his image of the artist in his relation to society, was undoubtedly Degas. And increasingly during the same years, the younger artist who came closest to sharing Degas's deeply conservative views and his cult of drawing as an instrument for concise, incisive commentary was Forain. Their affinity seems all the more remarkable when one considers the difference in their ages — Degas was born in 1834, Forain in 1852 — and the distance that separated them socially: Degas came from a cultivated Parisian family of bankers and brokers, many of whom maintained the aristocratic particle in their names, and Forain from a family of artisans and small shopkeepers with little formal education in provincial Reims.

When and under what circumstances the two artists first met is not known. The biographical sources on Forain place their meeting in 1874 and link it to the rejection of what was apparently the first work he submitted to the official Salon. "In 1874," Charles Kunstler relates, "Forain sent to the Salon a still life of a packet of biscuits framing a bottle of maraschino, which was rejected by the jury. Thanks to this failure and to his recalcitrant spirit, he was admitted into the magic circle of independent artists: Manet, Degas, the engraver Desboutin...."[1] A more exalted version of the same story is given by Jean Puget: "The next year [1874], the Salon jury rejected another of his still lives; this time a bottle of maraschino beside a packet of biscuits. His failure was greeted

with much acclaim by the Independent artists around Monet and Degas."[2]

These sources, like most of the others on Forain, are based on his recollections some fifty years later, when, on the eve of his death, the then-famous artist tended to dramatize and glorify his modest beginnings. It is hard to believe that the rejection of an insignificant picture by an unknown painter, one of the thousands routinely rejected by the Salon jury, would have attracted the smallest notice in a group of independent artists who were themselves long inured to rejection. But 1874 was a symbolically significant year for Forain, witnessing not only his first attempt to exhibit at the Salon, but also the first attempt by the artists who were soon to become known as the Impressionists to show their work collectively. Since Degas had played a major part in the organization of that show, it would have been natural for Forain to link these events as he recalled them half a century later.

The documentary evidence suggests that, on the contrary, the two artists met several years later and in more banal circumstances. When Degas moved to a studio on the rue Fontaine in 1877, he began frequenting the café La Rochefoucauld, just down the street. Among the other habitués was the young Forain, who worked in the same *quartier*,[3] and it was undoubtedly there that they met. The exalted acclamation of the rejected young artist is absent from this version, but the beginning of a long friendship based on congeniality and respect is clearly present. That they met in the late 1870s is confirmed by the fact that, although the Impressionists had held group exhibitions in 1874, 1876, and 1877, Forain first exhibited with them, at Degas's invitation, in 1879. And even then Forain wavered at first about doing so; according to Degas himself, "Manet managed to persuade a woman who was having her portrait painted by Forain that Forain's place was not with us. Amen to little Forain."[4] The date of their meeting is also confirmed by Degas's notation of Forain's addresses in his notebooks, all of them in the period 1878-1884.[5]

From the beginning of their friendship, Forain admired Degas to the point of veneration and was proud to proclaim it. Shortly before his death, Forain received a visit from Daniel Halévy, who as a young man had also known Degas well and was now gathering his letters for an edition he hoped to publish. In the course of sharing memories of the great man,Forain confessed quite simply: "Everything I am....I owe to him. Fifty or so years ago, I had somewhat anarchic tendencies. He uttered a few words to me.... And that was that."[6] Equally touching is the writer Pol Neveux's memoir of the aged Forain: "Calmly, speaking in a monotone voice, with the assurance of a well-behaved schoolboy pronouncing a lesson learned by heart, he recited the teachings of «Monsieur» Degas, piously stored in his memory. Infallible dogma, which «Monsieur» Degas had told him on the aims of the artist; articles of faith, his praise of finish; sacred words, the old man's invective against the defectors from realism, the bandits of Primitivism, the archaizing artists, the gregarious, the tamed."[7]

The power of Degas's example was indeed such that it helped the young Forain to form his public persona, or at least confirmed and encouraged the development of certain traits of his personality — the sharp, sarcastic, deliberately rude manner for which he became, like Degas, both renowned and feared. At the time of the Dreyfus Affair, it was again the example of Degas, whose violent anti-Semitism was widely reported, that confirmed Forain in his own anti-Dreyfusard views. Degas's role in his disciple's development was recognized by their contemporaries. Thus the poet Fernand Gregh, a friend of Daniel Halévy, remarked in his memoir of Degas: "He spoke brusquely; he overflowed with scathing expressions about his contemporaries, artists or others, and with remarks about life, of a picturesque cruelty which he had taught to Forain."[8] In this subject, however, Forain had little need of instruction, since such sarcasm came to him naturally. "His is a joyless spirit, ferocious and brutal," observed the poet Henri Ghéon, not without cruelty himself, "undoubtedly French, Parisian, working-class, yet full of rebelliousness and hatred."[9]

What such characterizations ignore, of course, is the gentler side of both men's personalities, their loyalty and devotion to old friends and their generosity to young, still unrecognized ones. But both men preferred to perform such acts of kindness privately, often even anonymously, while maintaining their harsher public demeanor.

As we have seen, "little Forain" himself was sometimes the butt of Degas's notorious "picturesque cruelty," at least at the beginning of his relationship with the older artist. Degas was both flattered and irritated by the extent to which his disciple's works resembled his own. "Forain paints with his hands in my pockets," he is reported to have said,[10] though he could have said the same about Mary Cassatt, Zandomeneghi, and others he had brought into the Impressionist circle and into their group exhibitions.

That Degas clearly recognized Forain's potential as well as his dependence, is evident from an account of an artists' dinner held in the spring of 1879, at the time he and Forain were first exhibiting together. Asked for his opinion of his "pupil," Degas replied: "Little Forain? He is still holding me by the coat tails, but he'll go far if he lets go."[11] One of the other artists who was present, foreseeing the same future for Forain, asked Émile Bergerat, editor-in-chief of a newly-founded, illustrated journal, reproachfully: "What? You don't have Forain at the *Vie Moderne?* Don't you know that one day he'll be a master who will be ranked between Daumier and Gavarni?"[12] From the second issue on, Forain did in fact contribute to this journal, but only vignettes and illuminated capitals, whereas Degas himself, Renoir, Cassatt, De Nittis, and less well-known artists published full-page drawings there. Forain had not yet become the famous caricaturist whose drawings, appearing on the front pages of the leading journals, were eagerly awaited and passionately discussed.

In one journal to be published in the early 1880s, however, Forain was invited to play a prominent part, and by Degas himself. For the first in a series of portfolios of original etchings, entitled *Le Jour et la Nuit,* which he hoped to sell to print collectors, Degas asked several artists who had participated in the Impressionist exhibition of 1879, among them Forain, to contribute large etchings reworked with aquatint. It was at this time, no doubt, that he wrote to Forain, urging him to complete his etching on time; and the collegial tone of his letter makes it clear that here, at least, he was not addressing "le petit Forain" but a respected colleague: "I wrote to you four days ago, my dear Forain, at the offices of the journal le Monde Parisien. You obviously didn't receive the letter, as I haven't heard from you. We need your plate *right now.* Answer me immediately....If you receive this in time to come this evening to Larochefoucauld, come at once."[13]

The same sense of cooperation among colleagues of equal stature is conveyed by the anonymous journalist who published a notice on *Le Jour et la Nuit* in January 1880: "Miss Mary Cassatt, Messrs. Degas, Pissarro, Forain, etc., get on very well together and are the best of friends. Never does any question of self-interest interfere with their fraternal feelings for each other."[14] And if this somewhat idealized view may not have been entirely accurate — may indeed have derived from an interview with Degas, seeking publicity for the new publication — in other newspapers of the time the individuality of

Forain's vision was clearly recognized, along with his evident dependence on Degas.

Thus the Italian critic Diego Martelli, reviewing the 1879 exhibition, noted perceptively: "Forain, a very young man, follows Degas with one foot and the caricaturist Grévin with the other. Despite that, his watercolors are stamped with originality, fruit of the young spirit and their creator's lack of constraint."[15] And the novelist and critic J.-K. Huysmans, who was already a friend of Forain's at this time, wrote of his works in the 1880 Impressionist exhibition: "A pupil of Gérôme, who taught him very little, Mr. Forain studied his art with Manet and Degas, which does not at all mean that he traces or copies their work; for he has a very individual temperament and a very distinctive vision of things."[16] Even Charles Ephrussi, an art historian and great admirer of Degas, remarked in his review of the 1881 Impressionist exhibition that "Forain, who has closely studied Degas's style, ...is able to give the actors in his little pieces a pointed wit that is utterly Parisian."[17]

Unfortunately, these early reviewers had neither the time nor the space to make clear what the similarities and differences between the two artists' works really were. Phrases like "stamped with originality" and "a very distinctive vision" testify to their awareness of such differences but remain vague generalities. And Huysmans, the most astute of contemporary observers and the one closest to Forain personally, could only resort to elaborate metaphors in attempting to specify what Forain learned from Degas about painting and how he made use of it. Contrasting Forain's very early work, archaic in its stiffness, with that of the late 1870s, Huysmans wrote in 1889: "Then that special flavor, hard, almost naïve, green, if one may say so, dissolved; under the influence of Mr. Degas, an altogether more complex technique appeared. He then made extraordinary watercolors heightened with gouache, backstage scenes and café-concerts, brothels and bars; he cooked stews of studiously spiced colors, put nudity in gourmet sauces, obtained unheard of effects by unexpected marriages and clashes of tone, achieved just the right nuance by attentively observing reflections and shadows, by using the exact science of additives and mixtures."[18]

Well into the twentieth century, critics and historians disagreed about the nature and extent of Forain's debt to Degas as a painter. When Forain's first retrospective exhibition, which included many watercolors and drawings that had not been seen for thirty years, was held at the Musée des Arts Décoratifs in 1913, reviewers expressed strongly opposed views, depending on their ideological positions. The avant-garde writer Henri Ghéon, contrasting the two major aspects of Forain's achievement, noted perceptively: "What has thus far inhibited the painter, and what will in fact enable the satirical cartoonist to develop, is that gift of moral observation which brings Forain closer to a writer such as Becque [a leading Naturalist playwright] than to a painter such as Degas. His first look is not at the «form», at the appearance of beings, but at the character and morals that the form will reveal. He follows Degas into the dancers' reception room, but with different intentions. Degas is ironic, as he is, but remains distant and calm; even if he is amused by what he hears, he has come to observe; neither anecdotes, gossip, nor colorful remarks distract him from his point of view, which is exclusively pictorial.... Forain is nervous, curious, without serenity; he moves from one group to another and lends an ear; he lip-reads conversations; when he can join in, he does so. He is still the Parisian waif in the street: he takes part in the life of the neighborhood; for life he forgets his art."[19]

An altogether different view was taken by Louis Gillet, the conservative curator of the Musée de Chantilly. Disdainful of the Naturalist writers' and certain Impressionist painters' fascination with the sordid side of modern urban life — and all the more so because Zola, the most prominent Naturalist, was also the most notorious Dreyfusard — Gillet denied Forain's affiliation with that school. "In practice, he does not accept the academic doctrine that art is superior to reality, and as a result he takes it as his duty to represent reality in the way required to disgust us with it. He differs on this issue with his master Degas; he avoids the abject forms, the intimate secrets, the hidden miseries, in which his famous, misanthropic friend delights; he feels no need to debase joy and hold it in contempt; he does not have that monastic hatred of the flesh: he rarely shows its repugnant aspects."[20]

Taking still another view, the noted critic and collector Arsène Alexandre, whose broad sympathies among the Impressionists included both Degas and Forain, insisted that all such comparisons were invalid. Speaking of Forain's "compositions based on backstage life and ballet at the Opera," he added: "In this respect one should avoid comparisons, really too facile and verging on banal error, with works of this kind by Mr. Degas and Toulouse-Lautrec. It would be so simple, though not within everyone's reach, to place side by side a picture of such a subject by each of the three artists. Yet how many people play this puerile and almost always false game of analogies! I have just mentioned Mr. Degas. Forain, himself inimitable, never dreamed of imitating this great man, for whom he expressed the deepest respect...."[21]

Recent art historians, benefitting from their longer perspective, have succeeded in defining the relation of Forain's work to Degas's in a more comprehensive and balanced way, beginning with the most obvious resemblance, in subject matter. As Alicia Faxon notes, both artists represented "dancers, the theatre, the race course and nudes in naturalistic interiors, often sharing the same model," but each chose certain subjects the other did not: "laundresses, modistes, and musicians" in Degas's work, "courtroom scenes, strikes and religious themes" in Forain's, at least after 1900.[22] And broadly speaking, Faxon adds, in treating these subjects "Degas was interested in fugitive appearances, movement and the purity of line, while Forain concentrated more on character, revealing gestures, social situations and the conversations and expressions of his subjects."[23] But that such a distinction may be too broad is suggested by the critic Félix Fénéon's use of some of the same terms to describe the works of both artists, as well as of their colleague Raffaëlli, at the Impressionist exhibition of 1886: "[They are] concerned above all with movement, with anecdote, and with character."[24]

It is, nevertheless, Ghéon's view, contrasting a "distant and calm" Degas at the Opera with a "nervous, curious" Forain, that has gained acceptance. Indeed, in comparing their treatments of the ballet dancer, Lillian Browse makes the same point as he, though in a less nuanced way: "Since the early seventies the *rats* de l'Opéra, as well as the *sujets* and *étoiles,* had been used by Degas with brilliant objectivity. His only real interest was in their relationship with ballet, the art that presented such an eternity of possibilities to his particular aesthetic and formal ideals, [whereas] Forain turned the subject of the dance to yet another use, that of social satire.... The pathetic plight of these young girls, the avarice of their mothers, the mean and heartless animal-greed of their 'admirers', were what Forain set out to flay."[25]

In much the same way, though with less sympathy for Forain, Fronia Wissman contrasts their treatments of another subject they shared, the actress in her dressing room: "Forain's *Loge d'Actrice* shows an actress in *déshabillé* staring out at the viewer, as her hairdresser turns to talk to the older man in evening clothes, the protector of the young woman. The contrast between the small, blond actress with her large, doe-like eyes, fingering some flowers on the dressing table, and the huge, black, buxom mass of the hairdresser, likewise fingering the actress's hair, verges on the farcical. In a work with a similar theme by Degas, *Avant l'Entrée en Scène,* for example, in which a seamstress mends a dancer's skirt while a male admirer looks on, the tone is serious and even somber. Forain makes explicit and anecdotal that which Degas leaves suggested and ominous."[26]

Comparisons such as these, focusing on subject-matter and content, have largely ignored what Forain learned from Degas's innovations in composition, style, and technique. Here the observations of Florence Valdès-Forain in the present catalogue, particularly with regard to Forain's fan paintings, are more pertinent. As she notes à propos of *Dancer with a Rose* (cat. no. 41), it was Degas who encouraged him to experiment with this unusual format and to send four fans to the 1879 exhibition; and Degas whose influence is evident: "The off-center position of the dancer at the left creates an asymmetrical effect...The ballerina is standing before a barely sketched landscape that recalls Degas's empty spaces." Similarly, in *Dancer in a Colored Tutu* (cat. no. 42), where "the lower left corner is vacant and the figure moves before a scarcely suggested setting, ...Forain is heavily influenced by Degas's style of leaving large areas of his fans uninhabited." In *Dancer* (Fan) (cat. no. 40), another compositional strategy, "the prominence and position of the stage flat derives directly from compositions Degas developed in his series of fans between 1878 and 1880." And if in this work, "in contrast to Degas, who covers certain fans with gold and silver dust, Forain is not seeking a decorative effect," but instead "is concentrating on a graphic effect," the study for *Ballet in a Garden* (cat. no. 39) "shows that the artist considered representing a night scene and using gold dust like Degas in some of his fans." The importance for Forain of Degas's technique is also evident in the beautifully executed *Woman with a Fan* (cat. no. 17): "Degas influenced

Forain to use the pastel technique after 1878, especially for portraits, and around 1885 for intimist scenes exalting femininity. The liveliness of touch and the immediate transcription of a sensation definitely indicate the teachings of Degas."

When, however, such comparisons are drawn to suggest the influence of Forain's style on Degas's, they seem less convincing. Thus Phylis Floyd, discussing Forain's watercolors, pastels, and drawings of the 1870s, argues that "the style of these small-scale works, marked by an expressive brushwork and exaggerated color, corresponds to Degas's experiments in graphic media during the second half of the decade, and the ascendancy of a more calligraphic facture in Degas's work of the time suggests the impact of his younger follower."[27] In fact this facture has its roots in Degas's own practice earlier in the decade, when he began treating studies, sketches, and pictures of small format — and not always observing clear distinctions among these — more freely than his larger, more ambitious compositions. On this subject, the observation by Huysmans cited earlier, "under the influence of Mr. Degas, an altogether more complex technique appeared [in Forain's work]," seems more just.

As the two men became better acquainted, the force and originality of Forain's personality, which had already gained him the friendship of many other artists and writers, including Manet, Cézanne, Rimbaud, Verlaine, and Huysmans, seem also to have charmed Degas. Writing in October 1883 to Henri Rouart, a friend and fellow artist who was then in Venice, Degas suggested that he visit the Palazzo Labia "to see, partly for yourself, partly for me, Tiepolo's frescoes." And he added, anticipating his friend's surprise, "Forain — yes, Forain — gave me a survey of these on the table at the Larochefoucauld café, a survey he finished by comparing them with a poster by Chéret."[28] Forain, who had presumably visited the Palazzo Labia on his recent trip to Italy,[29] may have been reminded of Chéret's popular posters by the light tonalities, foreshortened figures, and theatrical costumes in Tiepolo's frescoes. With a kind of grudging respect, Degas concluded: "That was his way of admiring them. It's perhaps no less valid than another way."[30]

Yet it was at just this time that Forain began to drift away from Degas and the Impressionist circle — artistically if not personally. Like Degas, he did not participate in their 1882 group exhibition; but unlike Degas, and despite the latter's strong disapproval, he began to exhibit at the Salon, showing *Le Buffet* in 1884 and *Le Veuf* in 1885.[31] Both in their larger, more ambitious scale and their tighter, more descriptive style, these works were influenced by such commercially successful painters of modern life as Tissot and De Nittis, who adapted Degas's innovations to popular taste. This shift in Forain's approach, which he himself heralded in a little-known interview with Jules Hoche in 1883 expressing his dissatisfaction with the Impressionist shows,[32] was also noted, with regret, by Pissarro a year later: "Forain apparently no longer works in the same style as before, from what I've been told; that's a great shame, since he does not lack a critical and very observant mind." And inevitably, Pissarro then compared Forain to Degas: "Between Degas and all the rest [he had also named Robida and Gauguin], there's a world of difference! It's just for show, nothing more."[33]

But if they diverged artistically in the later 1880s, Degas and Forain drew closer personally. Writing in October 1890 to Ludovic Halévy, a playwright and old friend, sending him the latest bulletin on his trip in a horse-drawn tilbury from Paris to Burgundy and back with the sculptor Bartholomé, Degas described with evident admiration the outspoken, colorful behavior of Forain, who had gone to Melun to greet them on their return and share a meal with them. "You don't give Brie like that to Parisians! Forain tells the waiter. He has arrived on his tricycle, in Garibaldian dress, and speaks of the fortunes of the bicycle. He is standing and speaking with a piece of food in his mouth."[34]

By then it was clearly the man more than the work that attracted Degas to Forain. As Paul Valéry, who first met Degas in 1894, recalled: "Degas had a great weakness for Forain. Forain would say: Monsieur Degas, as Degas would say: Monsieur Ingres. They would exchange their devastating remarks."[35] Not surprisingly, then, their extant correspondence (carefully preserved on Forain's side, lost or destroyed on Degas's) dates almost entirely from the 1890s and is almost entirely concerned with arrangements for dining together.[36] This was of course the decade of the Dreyfus Affair, which divided the group of former Impressionists as it divided the whole of French society, with Monet and Pissarro on one side, Renoir and Cézanne, as well as Degas and Forain, on the other, though the last two were more vehement in denouncing the officer whom they felt had betrayed the army and the nation, institutions they revered, and who moreover was Jewish, a group they reviled.[37] Thus Degas's letters to Forain are generally about plans for dinner at his home or at the homes of Baron Cochin or Countess Potocka, in the company of General Mercier, Maurice Talmeyr, and others with reactionary and anti-Semitic views.

One of Degas's letters, however, is about a drawing by Forain. Written in April 1898, shortly after Forain's "Cassation" appeared in the anti-Dreyfusard journal *Psst...!,* which he himself published with the caricaturist Caran d'Ache, the letter reads: "Forain, my noble friend, how handsome your latest drawing is! And no caption. Annulment is enough. The head is magnificent. So many things can be expressed in drawing!"[38] The *cassation* (annulment) in question was of a verdict handed down two months earlier that found Zola guilty of libelling the Army in his famous open letter "J'accuse." That Degas and Forain had both

known the writer well and shared his Naturalist views of modern urban subject-matter in the 1870s hardly mattered to them by then, though a friend of Forain's recalled that he "was greatly impressed by the article, which he read out to me with admiration for the author...."[39] Indeed the writer they both now found more congenial was Maurice Talmeyr, the brilliant and vehemently anti-Dreyfusard journalist and novelist, whom Degas asks Forain in the same letter to invite for dinner.

Apart from its ideological content, "Cassation" also appealed to Degas as a drawing of exceptional force and eloquence. So impressed was he by Forain's drawings at this time, in the mass-circulation *Le Figaro,* as well as the short-lived *Psst...!,* that he routinely saved them. "In the living room, furnished in late Louis-Philippe style," his friend Paul Lafond recalled, "on a table in the middle of the room were piled up issues of *Le Figaro* containing Forain's weekly drawings, which Degas appreciated in a very special way."[40] These reproductions of drawings did not of course figure in the posthumous sales of Degas's collection, but the latter did contain thirteen drawings and a monotype by Forain and one relatively late painting of a courtroom scene.[41] They confirm what was already known, that it was Forain the draftsman, and especially the satirical draftsman, whom Degas admired; but they also suggest the limits of his admiration. Compared to the number and importance of the works in Degas's collection not only by his predecessors Ingres, Delacroix, and Daumier, but also by his contemporaries Manet, Cézanne, and Gauguin, these small drawings by Forain form a modest group — one that hardly supports Browse's assertion that "among the fine works of art that he had bought when his finances permitted, [Degas] could rarely resist buying a Forain."[42]

Degas's admiration for Forain's political satires of the late 1890s is hardly surprising, since it was in these works that his genius for drawing, the very aspect of his work that would have meant most to Degas, finally appeared in all its power. As Kunstler puts it, "He draws on the paper forceful contours and broad gashes. His line, thin at the beginning, grows thicker. The soft pencil, the pen, or the brush that he uses indiscriminately spread out furiously on the paper or the [lithographic] stone, press down hard wherever they land, as if they were crushing an evil creature."[43]

It was this notion of the incisiveness of drawing, its capacity to cut through appearances to expose the deeper truth beneath, in short, its sharp-edged moral probity, whether in treating the hypocrisy of daily life or what both artists considered the betrayal of traditional values, that they shared. At the same time, this openly aggressive kind of drawing was in both cases the natural means of expression of a personality that was uncompromising and outspoken in its moral rectitude, at times mocking or cruel in denouncing what it blindly opposed. What Forain later recalled of his prevailing mood at the time of the Dreyfus Affair was equally true of his friend Degas's, though the latter refrained from politicizing his art: "Forain says that, in those troubled times, he would go to bed in a state of rage and get up, after a feverish sleep, still more enraged."[44] And for both artists, who of course could also draw with subtlety and grace when the subject and their mood required it, the aggressive potential of drawing forcefully and incisively made it an ideal outlet for that "state of rage."

So it was appropriate that the aged Degas should have wished for no other eulogy at his funeral than the brief one he wanted his fellow draftsman to deliver: "You, Forain, will say, 'He greatly loved drawing: so do I,' and you will go home."[45]

Endnotes

[1]Charles Kunstler, *Forain*, Paris, 1931, p. 16.

[2]Jean Puget, *La vie extraordinaire de Forain*, Paris, 1957, p. 39.

[3]Paul Lafond, *Degas*, Paris, 1918, p. 89; Gabriel Astruc, *Le pavillon des fantômes*, Paris, 1987, pp. 87-88: both cited in Henri Loyrette, *Degas*, Paris, 1991, pp. 338-339.

[4]Letter to Caillebotte, March 1879; quoted in Marie Berhaut, *Gustave Caillebotte, sa vie et son oeuvre*, Paris, 1978, p. 243. In a notebook list of potential participants in the show, Degas had at first included Forain's name, then cancelled it; see Theodore Reff, *The Notebooks of Edgar Degas*, 2nd ed., New York, 1985, Notebook 31, p. 93.

[5]Reff, *Notebooks of Edgar Degas*, Notebook 30, p. 215 (used in 1878-83); Notebook 33, p. 11v (used in 1879-82); Notebook 34, p. 225 (used in 1880-84).

[6]Daniel Halévy, *Degas parle*, Paris, 1960, pp. 154-165, journal entry of 14 November 1930; see also pp. 165-168, journal entry of 15 December 1930: the account of a second visit, with further reminiscences of Degas.

[7]Pol Neveux, "Jean-Louis Forain," *Revue de Paris*, vol. 38, August 15, 1931, p. 790.

[8]Fernand Gregh, *L'âge d'airain, souvenirs 1905-1925*, Paris, 1951, pp. 11-12; cited in Loyrette, *Degas*, p. 519.

[9]Henri Ghéon, "Jean-Louis Forain," *Art et Décoration*, vol. 33, January 1913, p. 6.

[10]Françoise Sevin, "Degas à travers ses mots," *Gazette des Beaux-Arts*, vol. 86, 1975, p. 28.

[11]Émile Bergerat, *Souvenirs d'un enfant de Paris*, III, Paris, 1913, p. 140, recounting a dinner given by De Nittis, at which Daudet, de Goncourt, Desboutin, and Manet were also present.

[12]See note 11.

[13]Undated letter, published by Henri Loyrette in *Degas inédit*, Paris, 1989, p. 387; there dated between December 1878 and May 1884, the publication span of *Le Monde Parisien*, but surely written in late 1879 or early 1880, when the preparations for *Le Jour et la Nuit* were most intensive. It was, moreover, only in 1879-1881 that Forain contributed to *Le Monde Parisien*.

[14]Anon., "Impressions d'un impressionniste," *Le Gaulois*, January 24, 1880; cited in Loyrette, *Degas*, p. 373.

[15]Diego Martelli, "Gli impressionisti, mostra del 1879," *Roma Artistica*, June 27 and July 5, 1879; quoted in *The New Painting: Impressionism, 1874-1886*, exh. cat., National Gallery of Art, Washington, D.C., 1986, p. 282.

[16]Joris-Karl Huysmans, "L'exposition des indépendants en 1880," in his *L'art moderne*, Paris, 1883, pp. 107-108.

[17]C. E., "Exposition des artistes indépendants," *Chronique des Arts et de la Curiosité*, 23 April 1881, pp. 134-135; quoted in *The New Painting*, p. 364.

[18]Joris-Karl Huysmans, *Certains*, Paris, 1928, p. 42; first published in 1889.

[19]Henri Ghéon, "Jean-Louis Forain," pp. 5-6.

[20]Louis Gillet, "Forain, son exposition aux Arts décoratifs," *Revue Hebdomadaire*, vol. 30, January 23, 1913, p. 487.

[21]Arsène Alexandre, "Forain tel qu'il fut," *La Renaissance*, vol. 14, January 1931, p. 285.

[22]Alicia Faxon, *Jean-Louis Forain, A Catalogue Raisonné of the Prints*, New York, 1982, p. 9.

[23]Faxon, *Jean-Louis Forain*, pp. 9-10; for further comparisons between the two artists, see pp. 41-43.

[24]Félix Fénéon, "Les impressionnistes en 1886," in his *Oeuvres plus que complètes,* ed. Joan Halperin, 2 vols., Geneva, 1970, I, p. 47; first published in 1886.

[25]Lillian Browse, *Forain the Painter, 1852-1931,* London, 1978, p. 78.

[26]Fronia Wissman, "Realists among the Impressionists," in *The New Painting,* p. 340. Forain's picture is illustrated in *The New Painting,* cat. no. 108; Degas's in Paul-André Lemoisne, *Degas et son oeuvre,* II, Paris, 1947, no. 497.

[27]Phylis Floyd, "Jean-Louis Forain," in *The Crisis of Impressionism,* exh. cat., Ann Arbor, 1980, p. 100.

[28]Letter of 16 October 1883; Edgar Degas, *Lettres,* ed. Marcel Guérin, 2nd ed., Paris, 1945, p. 72.

[29]One source places this trip in 1882 (Kunstler, *Forain,* p. 20), and another in the spring of 1883 (Léandre Vaillat, *En écoutant Forain,* Paris, 1931, p. 135). The two artists' admiration for Tiepolo's frescoes seems the more remarkable when we recall, first, that Degas never visited Venice and, second, that their admiration was not widely shared at the time. On contemporary opinions of the frescoes, see Michael Levey, *Giambattista Tiepolo, His Life and Art,* New Haven and London, 1986, p. 143.

[30]See note 28.

[31]Illustrated in Browse, *Forain the Painter,* pls. 15 and 16.

[32]Jules Hoche, *Les Parisiens chez eux,* Paris, 1883, p. 201; cited in Richard Thomson, "Jean-Louis Forain's 'Place de la Concorde': A Rediscovered Painting and Its Imagery," *Burlington Magazine,* vol. 125, March 1983, p. 157.

[33]Camille Pissarro, letter to Lucien Pissarro, 1884; his *Correspondance,* ed. Janine Bailly-Herzberg, I, Paris, 1980, pp. 285-286.

[34]Letter of October 18, 1890; Degas, *Lettres,* p.173. Melun is of course in the heart of the Brie region.

[35]Paul Valéry, *Degas, danse, dessin,* Paris, 1938, pp. 128-129.

[36]Eight such letters are published by Henri Loyrette in *Degas inédit,* Paris, 1989, pp. 385-387. It is true that Degas saved very few of any correspondent's letters.

[37]See Loyrette, *Degas,* pp. 638-648, and Faxon, *Jean-Louis Forain,* pp. 21-22.

[38]Letter of 9 April 1898, reproduced in Yves Brayer, "Forain le peintre que j'ai connu," *Gazette des Beaux-Arts,* vol. 91, 1978, p. 196. Forain's drawing had appeared in *Psst...!* that morning.

[39]"Memoirs of the Late Princesse Edmond de Polignac," *Horizon,* vol. 12, August 1945, p. 117.

[40]Lafond, *Degas,* p. 118.

[41]Sales of Collection Edgar Degas: Galerie Georges Petit, Paris, March 26-27, 1918, nos. 38, 166-176; Hôtel Drouot, Paris, November 6-7, 1918, no. 122; Hôtel Drouot, Paris, November 15-16, 1918, nos. 172, 173.

[42]Browse, *Forain the Painter,* p. 65.

[43]Kunstler, *Forain,* p. 32.

[44]Jacques-Emile Blanche, "Jean-Louis Forain," *Essais et portraits,* Paris, 1912, p. 72.

[45]Various versions have been reported. This one is quoted in *Forain,* exh. cat., Roland, Browse and Delbanco, London, 1964, p. 3.

A Portrait of Jean-Louis Forain

by his great granddaughter Florence Valdès-Forain

"I was born in Reims on the 23rd of October 1852 and I adore Ballet."[1] This was the laconic reply given by Jean-Louis Forain (1852-1931) to the newspaper *Le Courrier Français* when asked to write his autobiography in 1888. At 36, he had been contributing to satirical journals for 12 years and was already a sought-after humorist. Although his talents as a painter were not yet acknowledged by the public at large, they were recognized within the intimate group of Impressionists with whom he had exhibited his works four times between 1879 and 1886.

Nevertheless, his reply is noteworthy because it reveals three character traits which run through the artist's entire life. First, Forain did not like to talk about himself. In old age, he remained tactfully discreet about personal matters, revealing few intimate details to his two biographers, Léandre Vaillat and Charles Kunstler. For instance, he never explained why he changed his first name Louis to Jean-Louis. When he became famous and enjoyed status as a highly honored member of the French Academy late in his life, he exhibited modesty and humility, especially toward his fellow painters. Although he exposed the dark hidden aspects of his contemporaries' souls in drawings appearing in *La Comédie Parisienne*,[2] paradoxically, he remained largely silent about his private life.

Secondly, the artist emphasized his cultural ties to his native city of Rheims where he spent a happy childhood in the bosom of a poor but close-knit family.[3] His hometown's famous cathedral helped nurture his instincts as a painter. "If I became an artist, I owe it to the statues of Reims,"[4] he told Pol Neveux. Forain was deeply affected when the city was ravaged by shelling during World War I.

Finally, Forain's reply revealed his great passion for ballet, which inspired many of his works. In depicting this theme, Forain used all the techniques dear to him - pencil sketches, oils, watercolors, engravings, and pastels. He expressed the pictorial styles so characteristically his own, from the social commentaries derived from the works of his Impressionist masters, Manet and Degas, to the development of his own style of Expressionism. If ballet dancers inspired him in the same way as they did Degas, it is certainly because at the Paris Opera he could best "capture" the female body in movement. Moreover, the world of entertainment was for Jean-Louis Forain the best place to observe social mores, insofar as it was a microcosm of mankind. He loved to stroll behind the scenes and into the ballerinas' and actresses' dressing rooms to catch their conversations and witness the effect they had upon their admiring, yet aging, "season ticket-holders" who supported them.

Readers of *Le Courrier Français*, who awaited each issue to smile or laugh at Forain's cartoons, were perhaps disappointed by his elliptical autobiographical comments. They would doubtlessly have welcomed more information about "their" humorist's personality and, in particular, his most distinguishing characteristic: his caustic wit.

Forain expressed a new, intense ferocity when he entered the field of political caricature in the 1890s, particularly during the Panama Canal scandal and the Dreyfus Affair. To some, his biting sarcasm appeared cruel, yet to others, he abandoned himself to middle-class conformity in his mature years by defending traditional values.

In reality, Forain's personality mirrored his works, which are complex and difficult to classify within his stylistic evolution. His dual career as humorist and painter, however, made him a worthy heir to Daumier.

Archives and family accounts provide

greater knowledge of the intimate Forain, the disconcerting and attractive figure of the "Belle Epoque." They reveal the hidden good nature of someone often considered a cynic, and the lifelong nonconformism of a defender of traditional values.

Gaiety and Cynicism Conceal Sensitivity

An examination of Forain through his self-portraits provides a revealing glimpse of the artist. These works are almost as numerous as those left by Rembrandt, whom Forain admired and copied many times. In *Self-Portrait with Beard,*[5] Forain's spirit emanates from the crease of his ironic lips and his piercing and sharply searching eyes. An obstinate lock of hair sweeps his high forehead. His caustic wit, his cutting remarks learned on the Paris pavement, and the street-talk picked up in Montmartre led the poets Verlaine and Rimbaud, to dub him Gavroche.[6] All his life, Forain remained that mocking Gavroche – impertinent, incorrigible, roguish – a man who made fun of anything, at times ferociously.

This spiritedness enabled Forain to endure his impoverished beginnings as an artist. Though his Rheims childhood was carefree, in his adolescence he encountered overwhelming setbacks. Arriving in Paris at the age of 11, the young Forain devoted himself to drawing. More inclined to copy the masters in the Louvre than to study at school, he was soon noticed by Carpeaux, the great "Second Empire" sculptor, who asked Forain to join his studio. However, his good luck did not last long and, at 17, Forain's life took an unhappy turn. He was expelled from Carpeaux's studio, and his furious father threw him out of the family home. From time to time thereafter, he lived in frightful hovels. To keep from starving, he painted portraits of the newly deceased. A still life of a bouquet of violets from this

period was never finished because he could not afford the necessary tube of ultramarine paint.

His ready wit gained him easy entry into the "Club Zutique"[7] and the "Vilains Bonshommes"[8] dinners, where Paris's rebel artists, who included Carjat[9] and the poet Cros,[10] would gather around Verlaine and Rimbaud. Moreover, this period was just as

The earliest known image of Jean-Louis Forain, c. 1865.

tumultuous for France, recently defeated by Germany[11] and wounded by the Commune,[12] as it was for young Forain, who signed some of his drawings with an irreverent "Zut" ("What the Hell"). At the Café Guerbois,[13] where Manet and Degas met with their followers, a very young Forain listened passionately to the feverish discussions on Art. The famous critic Gustave Geffroy described Forain as "the mischievous imp whose jokes tickled his elders."[14]

While with his friends on the terrace at the Café Tortoni,[15] he would make do with a "Spanish-style drink" (a euphemism at the time for a free glass of water). Forain, nonetheless, owned a tail coat and certainly dressed stylishly. Like Picasso a few decades later, Forain did not hesitate to pay his tailor for a suit with a painting.[16] When he achieved financial success, he bought his clothes from the best tailors in the Place Vendôme and Bond Street, vying in elegance with his writer-friend Maurice Talmeyr.[17] Yet when he was young and penniless, it was as much out of necessity as out of interest in being smartly dressed that Forain went without basic necessities in order to afford tails. The latter were indispensable for attending the Opera and the receptions hosted by the Parisian high bourgeoisie. Forain wanted to observe that privileged society,[18] and he depicted it in fine works of art such as *Woman with a Fan* (cat. no. 17).

In presenting him with the academician's sword[26] the Minister for Arts, Bérard, accurately described Forain's art of conversation "...you seem absorbed in ironic

Forain loved night life and relished evenings out. In years to come, dinners, costume balls, evenings at the Jockey Club and the Cercle de l'Union Artistique would fill his appointment book. Immortalized by Sem[19] on the walls of Maxim's,[20] Forain enjoyed his own reserved table there. As evidence of his appetite for evenings out, here is an excerpt from a letter written around 1900 by his wife Jeanne to their young son, Jean-Loup: "Your Papa talks, whistles and sings, goes to put on his tail coat. He is tired out but I'm sure he'll have me going to sleep at two in the morning..."[21] That fashionable circles sought after Forain's presence as much as his artist-friends did, attests to the agile mind and the social intelligence of this artisan's son. More than 50 years of friendship bound him to Degas, who time and time again requested the presence of Monsieur and Madame Forain.[22] In Bonnard's painting, *Dinner at Vollard's*,[23] Forain, a frequent guest of the famous art dealer,[24] is depicted with Odilon Redon, the art collector Kessler and Misia Edwards.[25]

meditation. Suddenly you join the discussion, you say what's on your mind in a voice and tone in the manner of an etching...; and everything in the discussion changes. Sometimes, it is a vigorous clarification which reconciles or disarms the opponents, sometimes it is a lightening outburst that shatters their dialectic reasoning. At times you enter the controversy only to show that it is vain. You have the knack of putting an end to all discussion. Your interruptions, by their breadth, simplicity of line, and forceful good sense, are reminiscent of Molière's famous retorts."[27]

Yet "Forain had nothing of a courtier in him," notes the painter Jacques-Emile Blanche.[28] Although he had a certain curiosity for socialites and elegant people, he saved his fearsome and critical judgement for his boisterous high life companions. His conversations were barbed with vicious remarks, but he was always forgiven because of his wit. He was both admired and feared. Aware of this, he allowed himself to say whatever he liked. People applauded, bedazzled, always believing that the comments were aimed at someone else, and while laughing, they were apt to comment: "Good old Forain!" The Academician Maurice Donnay recalled that one day a famous banker told Forain "You're very nasty, so why does everyone always say 'Good old Forain?'" Forain replied, "My dear Baron, you know that everyone always says 'Poor old Rothschild!'"[29]

"When he thought of a witty remark, he couldn't keep it to himself," Jeanne Forain reminisced. She remembered that during a dinner, an actress who had not resigned herself to her grand old age, declared that she would put a gun to her head when she felt herself getting old. Forain murmured "Shoot." Then there was the time when a painter had just married one of his models whose nude portraits appeared in a large number of exhibitions. Forain considered her as the wedding party left the church and remarked, "She also looks good in a dress." His celebrated wit knew very few limits. Concerning the novelist Muhlfeld's widow who proudly paraded her recent conversion to Catholicism, he said, "She hasn't known the Blessed Virgin a week and she already calls her Mary!"[30]

Many anecdotes ascribed to Forain made the rounds: "The remarks! All sorts have been attributed to me," he confided to Charles Kunstler. "Absolutely untrue stories have been spread. Didn't they even go so far as to claim that Carpeaux and I were homeless together! But Carpeaux was 25 years older than I, and he was at the height of his fame when I met him."[31]

While his peers were the victims of his biting comments, Forain never attacked the needy. In Forain's presence, someone mentioned a hard working but poor journalist who borrowed small sums of money and never repaid them. Forain replied gravely "There are sums that one dares not repay."[32] Raised in the harsh school of poverty, he always showed himself to be compassionate to the deprived and the unfortunate. On the other hand, his experience did not make him lenient towards vain members of the bourgeoisie and corrupt politicians. His remarks, captions, drawings and certain of his paintings display an acute, dramatic vision, although never vengeful or grimacing. For example, when he painted a backstage scene, such as *Intermission. On Stage* (cat. no. 8), Forain denounced the social conditions suffered by the dancers who were obliged to prostitute themselves in order to survive. The contrast between the opulent, somber mass of season ticket-holders and the frail silhouettes of the ballet dancers clearly indicates his moralist message. Forain condemned these "protectors" who took advantage of the dancers' precarious situation.

Social injustice armed his hand with an incisive pencil when he drew a poor fellow bellowing, "What's the matter with the brat, bawling like that?" And his wife answers, "He's like us, he's hungry."[33] Or the small-minded bourgeois woman who addresses her manservant, "Where are the children?" "The young ladies are playing in the hall." "Go and tell the governess to make sure that the teacher's daughter doesn't play with the new doll."[34]

Although a harsh historian of social behavior, Forain did not alter reality: "I neither distort nor invent, I refract and for the good of everyone, I denounce.[35] I am not a caricaturist, I am a painter of reality: I copy."[36]

As Paul Léon so accurately stated in his funeral eulogy to Forain: "It was because of his pity for the victims, the humble people, the have-nots that he was ferocious with the others, the well-off, the conceited. Behind the mask of appearances, this humorist was tenderhearted. This skeptic was a patriot, this disillusioned man a believer."[37]

Just like Victor Hugo's Gavroche, a witty and cheerful waif, a Parisian with a heart of gold, Forain was generous. In his congratulations to the future Madame Forain (1865-1954), the painter Roger Jourdain wrote: "That she is marrying a man of wit, everyone knows. But what I am convinced of, and what I congratulate her for, is that she is marrying a good man."[38]

The episode at Carpeaux's studio illustrates his noble heart. As an adolescent, Forain worked with the famous sculptor. One day, an unlucky apprentice stumbled over the statue *Le Prince imperial et son grand chien (The Imperial Prince and his Great Dog)*. The Master, whose touchy character terrorized his pupils, flew into a fearsome rage and asked that the person responsible make himself known. "It is I,"[39] said the young Forain sadly, aware that the guilty party was a family man. Thus, Forain was expelled from Carpeaux's studio, and his future as a sculptor was dashed.

Another episode attests to the devotion that he had for his friends. In July 1914, a few days before the Great War broke out, Forain traveled to Leipzig to lend his support to the Alsatian humorist Hansi, who

Newlyweds Jean-Louis and Jeanne Forain in their home, 1892.

was brought before the High Court for his anti-German views. Forain wanted the sentenced man to be comforted by the view of a Frenchman, a friend, and member of the family of Cartoonists, and he clasped him in his arms. He then went to Colmar to reassure Hansi's father.[40]

Louis Morin, another member of the Society of Cartoonists of which Forain was president, recalled that the Cartoonists had "seen him a hundred times come to the aid of the most humble painters and the most destitute of old women, immediately, without hesitation."[41] Letters of thanks, such as the one from his friend Matout, show his kindness. But, like Degas, Forain kept these acts of kindness to himself, and Madame Forain learned about some of them only after his death.[42]

Forain revealed his sensitivity in touching scenes of motherhood.[43] For example one of his poignant World War I illustrations depicts a young mother with her face not visible who watches a soldier leaving. She says, "You see, my child, I'm not crying."

The beautiful love letters that Forain sent his future wife, Jeanne Bosc, whom he had met at Louise Abbema's studio, were sometimes illustrated with winged cherubs or various figures, and full of subtle gentleness. "It is raining, night has fallen and you are not coming. If I don't tell you how unhappy it makes me, it's because I'm afraid to annoy you with overly tragic tones. The other evening, I laid bare my heart because I couldn't help it. You spoke to me so kindly, in such a *virile* way, that no matter what I did, I couldn't hold back my tears. And I cried, painfully, over my incoherent life, over the energy that I dissipate instead of concentrating, and over the worthless results of my nonetheless real artistic efforts."[44]

In the same way, it was with intense emotion that Forain described to Jeanne on

Jean-Louis Forain and his three year old son, Jean-Loup, in his studio, 1898.

August 21, 1904, the demonstrations of faith that he witnessed during one of his pilgrimages to Lourdes and that served as inspiration for a series of etchings: "I no longer know how I live. In the two days that I've been here, I wander through the crowds of pilgrims, among the sick, with a lump in my throat, tears in my eyes; All the woes are there....I am feverish and aching from the sight of them. The sobs choke you, the tears stream from your eyes...."[45]

Traditionalism and Nonconformism

After spending Christmas 1900 with his old friend, the writer and art critic J.-K.

Huysmans,[46] at the abbey of Ligugé, Forain decided to use his art in the service of his faith: "I know that I shall not rest until I express my faith with the means that God gave me."[47] From that moment on, he painted religious compositions illustrating the Gospel, and wrote cartoon captions in support of the Church, which was threatened by anti-clerical legislation.

A fervent nationalist, supporter of the French homeland and the Army, he sorely deplored the loss of Alsace and Lorraine.[48] His patriotic campaign reached a high point with the drawings published during the First World War and collected in the *De la Marne au Rhin (From the Marne to the Rhine)* album.[49] Thus, in just a few decades, the twenty-year old anarchist, Communard sympathizer and welcome guest at the republican evenings given by Nina de Callias,[50] came to side with the traditionalists because the values to which he was strongly attached, such as those of the Nation and the Church, were now in danger.

Forain and his wife race in the Paris-Berlin car competition, 1901.

Forain's letters to his son Jean-Loup (1895-1941) clearly demonstrate these deeply patriotic feelings. Even though he showed much tenderness towards his son, Forain did not hesitate to remind Jean-Loup of his duty during his military service in December 1913. When his son was severely punished by his superiors, Forain sided with the Army, "Your punishment, however severe, is well deserved ....You must realize that what happened to you has distressed us greatly and that your mother loses sleep over it."[51] On June 24, 1915, he wrote to his son who had been seriously wounded: "I hope that you will make a complete recovery, and be in top form to give our country your very best."[52]

Forain became the standard bearer of traditional values. As a recognized artist, he consorted with the moneyed set and outwardly shared its way of life. In point of fact, the poverty that Forain had experienced in the 1870s gradually disappeared during the following decade, thanks to the growing income received from French newspapers, as well as from his British and American[53] patrons, who were among the first to recognize his talent as a painter. When the newspapers[54] announced his marriage in 1891, he was sufficiently well off to support his new household. By the turn of the century, Forain was a wealthy man. His fortune did not compare, of course, with that of the Vanderbilts and other American millionaires,[55] who invited him to their sumptuous homes when he visited the United States in 1893. Yet by 1899, Forain had his own private mansion built in Paris,[56] and in 1909, he acquired a country house near Versailles. He employed several servants and indulged in his taste for travel and new inventions such as the automobile and the telephone. This taste for progress earned him a barb from Degas, "So Forain, they ring you! And you run...,"[57] after he proudly told his friend that he was one of the first telephone subscribers in France.

However, in keeping with his bohemian temperament, he remained entirely emancipated from bourgeois conventions. Although very close to his wife and son, his family was unlike the traditional French family of 1900. It is surprising to read how freely he expressed himself to his son. Always prone to fanciful ideas, the Forains were not in the least bit averse to taming a parrot and a monkey. "Here (at home),

Jean-Louis and Jeanne Forain, c. 1894.

madness rules with the parrot and the monkey which at night has but one idea - to get into my bed, then hang on to my hair as soon as I try to catch him."[58]

Of course, the bourgeoisie, the cartoonist's favorite target, were never spared. "The other three guests are terribly bourgeois."[59] This sentence from a letter written at Plombières in 1894 is highly indicative of Forain's abhorrence of the pettiness and conformism of this environment.

"I shall marry you when you wake up... at noon."[60] This is the gentle ultimatum uttered by the pretty Jeanne to her fiancé, an incorrigible nighthawk, who stayed late in newsrooms and drew his inspiration from performances at the Opera, cabarets and bars. Madame Forain succeeded in tempering her husband's bohemian life, but he kept his nighttime habits and never worked early in the morning. "You see," he explained to Labrouche,[61] "mornings are for sleeping."[62]

The studio that he set up on the top floor of his house was spacious, but it seemed small to his visitors because it was so cluttered with drawings, canvases and sketches. In fact, this clutter provides an insight into Forain's creative process: his easel paintings were always surrounded by pencil sketches, because he never painted from life, with the exception of a few por-

Jean-Louis and Jeanne Forain in their studio in 1892. The two men on the left are unidentified. The oil painting of the young girl in front of Jeanne is by Jeanne. On the wall, the oil painting is by Jean-Louis, *Jeanne Forain in a Black Hat* (1891).

traits. Similarly, his satirical works were never drawn from nature, but were built from movements and attitudes that he recorded in one of the small notebooks he always carried with him. More importantly, they were also drawn from his astonishing memory. Like Hokusai, "the old man mad about drawing," Forain spent his life untiringly sketching lines on innumerable pieces of paper that piled up in his studio until he reached the economy of line so typical of his artistic gift. Once this was achieved, his characters spoke, contrary to some draughtsmen such as Gavarni,[63] who wrote their texts first and then made them fit the drawing. Forain's drawings dictated their captions. "I may find my caption first, but usually I make my drawing, then I listen to it," Forain explained to Arsène Alexandre.[64]

Finding the captions required a weekly, sometimes bi-weekly production, depending on political developments. Despite Forain's naturally creative mind, his newspaper work took up too much of his time and sometimes forced him to abandon his easel. After nearly half a century of newspaper illustrations[65] and thousands of published drawings, Forain sent his last drawing to *Le Figaro* in 1925 and, with relief, devoted the rest of his life to painting. The mysterious force that enabled him to rise from poverty never vanished. He was addicted to his art and produced a prolific and diverse body of work.

The studio was his territory, to which only a chosen few gained access. At the height of his talent, when Vuillard portrayed him in his studio,[66] he had no qualms about sending away unwanted visitors, including art dealers. His disinterest in the monetary aspect of his artistic production often disappointed enthusiasts eager to talk to him or obtain an autograph.

This rather short[67] but brilliant man was the only person able to impress the young Rimbaud[68] whose portrait he painted during their turbulent youth. However, in daily life, his wife saw him as a peaceable, relaxed and well-balanced companion. He was indeed fortunate to have a stable and harmonious marriage.

The happy and impish Jeanne was a good match for her husband's wit at Parisian dinners. In private, they were united by a strong complicity. He liked to share his taste for poetry with her. In the morning, he would recite verses by his favorite poets, Baudelaire, Rimbaud and Verlaine. Since he did not attend school for long, he learned poetry through writers,[69] friends from his youth. Every evening, he would read to his beloved, at the foot of her bed. His memory was such that when he closed the book, he could recite entire passages by heart.

A sweet and bright companion, Jeanne was the painter's favorite partner. A painter herself, she was able to understand not only his passions but also his creative anguish. They shared their admiration for works by other artists. She would often stay with him late at night when he was struggling with a caption, and with just one word, she could inspire him to find the right phrase. He was proud of his wife's art, giving her advice and encouragement, and, in 1921, he had an exhibition of his works alongside of hers.

Although the Forains were an extremely close-knit couple, they nonetheless remained fairly independent. Madame Forain would sometimes work alone in her studio on a child's face, her favorite subject, while her husband lunched or dined out in town.

Jeanne spent 40 years of her life devoted to him, and when he died, she withdrew into quiet retirement. Left alone with his memory, she modeled in clay her late husband's features which remained engraved in her heart. Once her sculpture was finished, she added the inscription: "FERVOR FECIT UXORIS (A wife's fervor made it).[70]

What a wonderful expression of love! A testament to make us regret all the more not having met this multifaceted individual named Jean-Louis Forain.

Endnotes

[1] J.L. Forain, Correspondence, dated November 25, 1888. *Le Courrier Français*, December 2, 1888, vol. 49, p. 3.

[2] *La Comédie Parisienne:* First Series published in 1892, Second Series in 1904.

[3] His father was a house painter, who specialized in signboards.

[4] "Jean-Louis Forain," *La Revue de Paris*, August 15, 1931, p. 775.

[5] *Self-Portrait with Beard,* pastel, 80 x 59 cm., c. 1885. Private collection.

[6] Gavroche was one of the main characters in Victor Hugo's novel *Les Misérables* (1862).

[7] The "Club Zutique" ("What the Hell" Club) was founded in October 1871 by Charles Cros (see note 10). The "Zutistes" met in a room at the "Hôtel des Etrangers." They kept a guest book called the "Album Zutique" which bears witness to the noisy ambiance of these meetings.

[8] The "Parnassian" poets, who included Banville, Leconte de Lisle, Coppée, Villiers de L'Isle-Adam, Catulle Mendès, and Sully Prudhomme, called themselves the "Vilains Bonshommes" (the "Bad Guys") and met every month.

[9] Etienne Carjat (1828-1906), the cartoonist and journalist, is well known for his photographs of contemporaries, in particular the writers Baudelaire and Mallarmé and the politician Gambetta. An anecdotal episode in Rimbaud's eventful life occurred when, after a "Vilains Bonshommes" dinner, the impetuous Rimbaud struck Carjat with a cane. Arthur Rimbaud, then 17 years old, was introduced by Verlaine at one of these dinners and he impressed the audience when he read his famous poem *Le Bateau ivre*.

[10] The poet Charles Cros (1842-1888) was a rather eclectic character since he also invented the phonograph (at the same time as Edison). His friends, Manet and Renoir, were enthusiastic about his experiments with color photography. His poems sometimes evoked the world of painters and were often dedicated to members of the Impressionist circle.

[11] The Franco-Prussian War, in which Napoleon III engaged in July 1870, led to the Emperor being captured at Sedan on September 2, 1870. This was followed by the rigors of the Siege of Paris, during which the people of Paris endured famine. The government's surrender on January 29, 1871, led to the loss of the French provinces of Alsace and Lorraine to Germany.

[12] The Commune was a revolutionary uprising led by Parisian workers in the wake of the German victory in 1871. The French government, which had withdrawn to Versailles, surpressed the insurrection with extreme brutality under leadership by Thiers. Although this civil war was shortlived (March 18th to May 28th), it nevertheless remains an important chapter in the history of proletarian revolution, and the bloody atrocities perpetrated by both sides (National Government and Communards) long remained ingrained in the collective memory of the French people.

[13] Located in the heart of Paris's "Batignolles" district, close to Manet's studio, the Café Guerbois was a focal point in the history of Impressionism. Manet met there on Friday evenings with his fellow painters, notably Whistler, Antonin Proust, Fantin-Latour, Alfred Stevens, and later on Degas, Renoir, Cézanne, Monet, Sisley, and Pissarro, and writers who embraced "Impressionist" ideas, such as Zola, Burty and Silvestre. The lively discussions led to the organization of a collective exhibition at the photographer Nadar's studio in 1874, which became the very first "Impressionist" exhibition. The Café Guerbois was gradually abandoned for the Café de La Nouvelle Athènes, in Montmartre, which was nearer to the studios of Degas, Renoir and Desboutin. Forain was also a regular visitor to "La Nouvelle Athènes."

[14] Charles Kunstler, *Forain*, Paris, 1931, p. 17.

[15]The Café Tortoni, on boulevard des Italiens, was also a meeting place for Manet's friends, especially during lunch. Edouard Manet appreciated the site's elegance where the "boulevardiers" would meet and exchange witty remarks. (The "boulevardiers" strolled the "Grands Boulevards" of the Right Bank, which became popular under Napoleon III and Baron Haussmann.)

[16]The work in question is *Le Buffet*, the first painting accepted at the Official Salon in 1884.

[17]While preparing for a dinner with Degas, he happened upon an old piece of mustard-colored fabric dating from the 1830s at his tailor's, Forain rubbed his hands. "Talmeyr won't have this one." But the tailor betrayed Forain, and Talmeyr turned up wearing an identical pair of pants. At first, Forain was furious, then both roared with laughter at the sight of the two pairs of "mustard" pants. Then Forain recounted how as a child his first pair of elegant breeches were discarded jockey pants. (Suzanne Barazetti, *Beaux-Arts,* no. 255, November 26, 1937).

[18]The Godillots, wealthy shoemakers, who appreciated both his art and wit, were Forain's first patrons. Later, other members of high society opened the doors of their prestigious salons to him, including Countess Potocka, Madame Bulteau, Countess Greffülhe, the Saint-Marceaux, the Cahen d'Anvers, Anatole France, etc. Having become very fashionable, he was a Parisian figure sought after by the great dandies Robert de Montesquiou and Boni de Castellane. He was a frequent guest of the Vogüe family and visited them regularly at the Château of Vaux le Vicomte. He also went on two cruises on the industrialist Pierre Lebaudy's yacht and was invited to the home of the banker's family Mendelssohn in Germany.

[19]Georges Goursat (1863-1934), known by the nickname of Sem, was a cartoonist famous for his descriptions of the Parisian high bourgeoisie before the First World War.

[20]A major meeting place of the "Belle Epoque," Maxim's was Paris's best known luxury restaurant, where high society and "demi-mondaines" such as Liane de Pougy, Caroline Otero and Emilienne d'Alençon would meet. This sophisticated establishment, with its Art Nouveau decor, is still located on rue Royale, close to Place de la Concorde.

[21]Undated letter written by Jeanne Forain to her son, Jean-Loup, c. 1900, Forain Family Archives.

[22] Telegram of January 30, 1902.

[23]*The Dinner at Vollard's* or *Vollard's Cellar, (Le Dîner chez Vollard* ou *La Cave de Vollard)* by Pierre Bonnard, c. 1907. Private collection.

[24]In a letter dated September 28, 1906, Vollard urged Monsieur and Madame Forain to accept his invitation to dinner. Forain Family Archives.

[25]Misia Godeska (1872 -1950), the ex-wife of Thadée Nathanson, who inspired the Nabis painters, became Madame Edwards before marrying the painter Sert.

[26]Elected in June 1924 to the Académie des Beaux-Arts (Fine Arts Academy), Forain was invested according to this prestigious institution's ritual. He received the academician's sword beneath the Institute's cupola, wearing a green suit, the ceremonial costume established by Napoleon I. The Académie des Beaux-Arts, located on quai de Conti in Paris, is made up of 50 painters, sculptors, architects, engravers and musicians. His election to the Institute was the crowning glory of Forain's career.

[27]*Bulletin de la Société des Dessinateurs Humoristiques*, no. 2, June 1924, p. 11.

[28]J-E Blanche, "Jean-Louis Forain," *Renaissance latine*, March 15, 1903, no. 3, p. 414.

[29] Maurice Donnay, "L'esprit sous la IIIe République," *Historia*, vol. 71, October 1952, p. 311.

[30] Jeanne Forain (1865-1954) conversations with her granddaughter Janine Chagnaud-Forain, the author's mother.

[31] Kunstler, *Forain*, p. 7.

[32] Pierre Labrouche, "Quelques souvenirs sur Forain," *Bulletin du Musée Basque de Bayonne*, vol. 21-22, 1943, p. 215.

[33] *Le Courrier Français*, March 8, 1896.

[34] J.L. Forain, *La Comédie Parisienne*, 2nd series, Paris, 1904, p. 116.

[35] Honoré Bostell, *Sous l'oeil de Forain*, Paris, 1958, p. 95.

[36] Donnay, *Historia*, p. 311.

[37] Speech by Paul Léon, member of the Institute and Director of the Ecole des Beaux-Arts (School of Fine Arts), delivered at Forain's funeral, July 15, 1931.

[38] Letter written by Roger Jourdain to Forain dated Tuesday, July 7, 1891, Forain Family Archives.

[39] Ch-M Widor, *Notice sur la vie et les traveaux de M. Jean-Louis Forain,* Institu de France, Académie des Beaux-Arts, Paris, 1931, p. 96.

[40] Speech by Hansi, *Bulletin de la Société des Humoristes*, vol. 2, June 1924, p. 6.

[41] Speech by Louis Morin, *Bulletin spécial de la Société des Humoristes*, n.d.

[42] An example is the letter of September 28, 1933, from the painter Jolibois, a mutual friend of Forain and Rimbaud.

[43] Drawn when he became a father in 1895.

[44] Undated letter from Jean-Louis Forain to his fiancée, Jeanne Bosc, c. 1890, Forain Family Archives.

[45] Forain Family Archives.

[46] Joris-Karl Huysmans (1848-1907), a fervent defender of the Impressionists, discovered Forain's talent in 1879. Their many common interests brought the art critic and painter together: they both expressed the same Naturalistic style, one with his pen, the other with his brushes. The most famous portrait of Huysmans is the one painted by Forain around 1878 (pastel, Musée d'Orsay, Paris, on loan from the Musée National du Château de Versailles, see fig. no. 24). The friendship between the two men grew stronger when Huysmans contributed to Forain's return to Catholicism.

[47] Letter dated January 5, 1901 from Jean-Louis Forain to Huysmans reproduced in *Le Figaro*, June 21, 1952, p. 5.

[48] See note 11.

[49] Mainly in the following newspapers: *Le Figaro, Oui, L'Opinion.*

[50] Nina de Callias (1845?-1884) opened up her salon to artists who lived unconventionally, such as Cézanne, Villiers de l'Isle-Adam, Desboutin, Verlaine, and Rimbaud, and revolutionary militants such as Vallès and Raoult Rigault. Nina de Callias, the poet Charles Cros's muse (see note 8), was also Manet's inspiration in several paintings of which the *Portrait de la Dame aux Eventails (Woman with Fans)* is the best known.

[51] Forain Family Archives.

[52] Forain Family Archives.

[53] Four of Forain's works were exhibited at the "Works in Oil and Pastels by the Impressionists of Paris" exhibition organized in New York by Durand-Ruel in 1886.

[54] "The marriage of Monsieur Forain, the well-known painter and illustrator, to Mademoiselle Bosc, a talented artist whose works at the Champ de Mars have been widely noticed, was celebrated yesterday at the town hall of the 8th arrondissement." *Le Temps,* July 19, 1891.

[55] At the invitation of Gordon Bennett, the wealthy owner of *The New York Herald,* Forain and his wife traveled for approximately six months throughout the United States, from April to October 1893.

[56] 30 bis, rue Spontini.

[57] Paul Valéry, *Degas, danse, dessin*, Paris, 1936, p. 1217.

[58] Letter from J.L. Forain to Jean-Loup Forain, dated February 6, 1914, Forain Family Archives.

[59] Letter from J.L. Forain to Jeanne Forain, c. 1894, Forain Family Archives.

[60] Janine Chagnaud-Forain's recollections of conversations with her grandmother, Jeanne Forain.

[61] "M'sieu" Labrouche helped Forain to print some of his engravings.

[62] Pierre Labrouche, *Quelques souvenirs sur Forain*, p. 216.

[63] Paul Gavarni (1804-1866) was a prolific cartoonist who criticized the bourgeoisie in newspapers such as *Le Charivari* and *L'Illustration.*

[64] Arsène Alexandre, *Du rire et de la caricature*, Paris, n.d., p. 320.

[65] He was nicknamed the "Juvenal" of the *Le Figaro*; Forain worked for almost thirty-five years for the famous Paris-based daily newspaper.

[66] *Souvenir d'une Dernière Visite à Forain (Recollection of a Last Visit to Forain)* Edouard Vuillard, oil, Musée Toulouse-Lautrec, Albi. Monsieur Antoine Salomon has informed us that Vuillard executed two portraits of Forain in 1927, now respectively in the Musée Saint Denis in Reims and in the San Francisco Museum of Modern Art. In November of 1938, Vuillard noted in his diary that he was reworking a third portrait of Forain. Soon thereafter, Vuillard donated this (third) portrait to the Albi museum.

[67] Forain was five feet, five inches tall.

[68] *Portrait of Arthur Rimbaud,* oil on canvas, 24 x 32.5 cm., dedicated: "May 1874 to my friend Poitelan." Private collection.

[69] See note 8.

[70] Shown at the Salon of the Société Nationale des Beaux-Arts in 1934, and donated by Jeanne Forain to the Académie des Beaux-Arts.

Jean-Louis Forain Chronology

1852
October 23, Jean-Louis Forain is born at Reims in Champagne, 100 miles east of Paris. His father was an ornamental sign painter; an uncle restored statues in the cathedral; some of his ancestors had been grape-growers.

1860
His family moves to Paris.

1866-67
The young Jean-Louis begins to draw at the Louvre. The painter Jacquesson de la Chevreuse gives him drawing lessons.

1868-69
He works for more than a year in the studio of the sculptor Carpeaux, then at the Ecole des Beaux Arts in the class given by Gérôme and finally with the caricaturist André Gill.

1870
Forain takes part in the defense of the fort of Montrouge, near Paris, against the Prussian soldiers.

1871-72
After the war, he returns to the Louvre; at that time he becomes the friend of Verlaine and Rimbaud.

1874
Portrait of Rimbaud. Forain completes his military service in the 101st Infantry at Laval.

1875
He returns to Paris very poor. His principle sources of income are the few illustrations turned out by small satirical newspapers which are the first to accept his works--*Le Scapin*, then *Le Monde Parisien, Le Café Concert, Le Chat Noir.*

1875-76
In Montmartre, at the Café de La Nouvelle Athènes, he meets Manet, Degas, and the art critic Huysmans, whose portrait he later makes (1878), and whose book *Marthe* he illustrates.

1879
Forain takes part in the 4th exhibition of Independent Artists (the Impressionists). He exhibits with Mary Cassatt, Degas, Monet, Pissarro, and others.

1880
He participates in the 5th Impressionist Exhibition. Among the exhibitors: Cassatt, Degas, Gauguin, Guillaumin, Pissarro, Raffaëlli and Berthe Morisot. In his critique of the exhibition Huysmans writes, "Forain has studied his art with Manet and Degas."

1881

Participates in the 6th Impressionist Exhibition, just before his first trip to Italy.

1884

For the first time a painting by Forain, *The Buffet*, is accepted into the official Salon. The following year he exhibits *The Widower* there.

1886

He takes part in the 8th and last Impressionist Exhibition. The art dealer Durand-Ruel exhibits Forain's canvases in New York along with those of Degas, Manet, Monet, Renoir, and Pissarro.

1886

Drawings by Forain are accepted by *Le Courrier Français* and *Le Figaro*. It is the beginning of an exceptionally fruitful collaboration: about 1,000 drawings, spread over forty years.

At this time, Forain has become a figure of Parisian life, sought after and feared by high society, which dreads and appreciates his *bons mots*. Nevertheless, he remains a bohemian, frequenting the backstages of theaters, the Opera balls.

Jean-Louis Forain, c. 1886.

1889

He undertakes in his satirical weekly, *Le Fifre*, "to recount everyday life and to show the sorrow of many joys." But it is a failure. For lack of money the journal lasts only four months.

Jean-Louis and Jeanne Forain on the ocean liner *La Bourgogne* which arrived in New York on April 19, 1893.

1890

He mounts his first one-man show at the Galerie Boussod-Valadon, which enjoys a great success.

1891

He marries a young woman of great beauty, Mlle. Jeanne Bosc, a painter, who little by little brings equilibrium and stability into his life. He makes several portraits of his young wife, notably *Mme. Jeanne Forain in a Black Hat*. He becomes a member of the Society of French Pastelists.

1892

Forain publishes the first volume of the *Comédie Parisienne*, a collection of social satire drawings which are always accompanied by captions of biting wit. From this period, Boulangism, Panama, the Dreyfus

Affair (1894-1900) orient him towards political satire; hundreds of drawings comment on events of the day - sometimes ferociously - in the dailies or the illustrated weeklies. Some of his political drawings were brought together into albums, such as *Les Temps Difficiles* (1893) and *Doux Pays* (1897).

This intense activity does not prevent Forain and his wife from making numerous voyages: Venice, Madrid, etc.

1893
The Director of the *New York Herald*, Gordon Bennett, invites Forain and his wife to the United States. They arrive in New York in April 1893 and are received by August Belmont, Whitney Warren, the Vanderbilts, and, of course, Bennett. The young couple go to Chicago where they stay at the Virginia Hotel and visit the World's Fair. They return to New York, leaving for France in October, after a stay of five months.

Sale of drawings at Georges Petit.

1895
Birth on May 11 of his only child, Jean-Loup.

Jean-Louis Forain, c. 1899.

1899
He builds a townhouse on the rue Spontini, near the Bois de Boulogne.

1900
Christmas Day at midnight mass in the abbey of Ligugé, Forain finds his old friend Huysmans. He returns from it "revived and gathered together for more worthy works of art..."

1904
Second volume of the *Comédie Parisienne*.

1900-05
At the dealer Vollard, he finds Degas, Cézanne and Renoir at the cellar dinners.

1905-10
Publication of a new series of etchings whose subjects are taken, for the most part, from the Gospel and the Bible. But, an intense worker, he still paints and engraves nudes and portraits: *Renoir* (1905) and *Madame de Noailles* (1910).

Exhibitions at the Bernheim Gallery 1906 and 1909.

1909
Forain rents, then buys, a country home at Le Chesnay, near Versailles.

1910
Takes part in the International Exhibition of Brussels.

Jean-Louis Forain during a weekend at his friends' castle.
The two ladies are unidentified.

1911
Exhibition in London at the Society of Painters, Sculptors and Engravers.

1912
Forain and his son are stretcher-bearers at Lourdes. He brings back a series of religious etchings.

1913
Very important one-man show at the Musée des Arts Décoratifs in Paris. It brings together 390 paintings, watercolors, drawings, lithographs, and etchings.

Cruise to seaports in the Levant.

1914-18
During the war with Germany, Forain puts his talent to the service of his country, notably in the columns of *Le Figaro* and *L'Opinion*.

In 1915, aged 62, he enlists in the Camouflage Section; simple soldier, then under-lieutenant, he is received as a friend by the great French military leaders, Joffré, Foch, Pétain. At the same time hundreds of war drawings, "of which some are worth a victory," were appearing in the papers. Later (1920), these drawings are gathered together in two volumes entitled *De la Marne au Rhine.*

1917
Forain is present - almost alone - at the burial of his friend Degas.

1918
The war over, Forain continues his collaboration with *Le Figaro* until 1924, but little by little he abandons his chalks for paint brushes. He paints cabaret scenes (*The Tango*), the law courts, episodes from the war (*The Relieving Troops*) and, more and more, often evangelical themes (*The Pilgrims of Emmaus, the Return from Calvary*), which haunt his mystical spirit.

1920
President of the Society of Humorists and of the Free Commune of Montmartre.

1921
Exhibition at the Trade Union of Fine Arts by Forain and Madame Forain.

1922
New cruise to the Levant with his son.

1923
He is elected a member of the Academy of Fine Arts.

1924
Represents France at the exhibition of Copenhagen.

1925
Forain is president of the National Society of Fine Arts. He represents the Academy of Fine Arts in Madrid.

1928
Commander of the Legion of Honor. Foreign member of the Royal Academy of Sweden.

1929
He exhibits at the 28th International Exhibition of the Carnegie Institute five paintings including *The Charleston, The Stockade*, and three scenes of law courts.

1930
Member of the Royal Academy of England. Trip to Barcelona. He returns to Lourdes for the last time. He continues to paint.

1931
He dies in Paris on July 11. In his funeral oration, Paul Léon says: "This ironist was a sensitive man; this sceptic was a patriot; this disillusioned one was a believer."

Janine Chagnaud-Forain

Reprinted with permission from:
Jean-Louis Forain: Artist, Realist, Humanist, International Exhibitions Foundation, Washington, D.C., 1982-1983.

CATALOGUE
OF THE
COLLECTION

Editor's Note
Many of the works created by Forain during his Impressionist years were untitled and undated. The titles and
dates in this catalogue reflect the consensus of the
authors. Measurements are given in inches and
centimeters, height preceding width.

1.

The Client

(Le Client ou Maison close)

Pencil, watercolor, and gouache
9 3/4 x 12 3/4 in. (24.7 x 32.8 cm.)
Signed and dated at u.r.: *Louis Forain / — 78*
1878

Now one of the most famous of Forain's early pictures — it appears, for example, as the frontispiece in the only monograph on his paintings[1] — *The Client* was largely ignored when it was first shown, *hors catalogue*, at the Impressionist exhibition of 1880. Among the reviewers, only Huysmans, a friend and strong supporter of the artist, discussed it at any length; but his discussion captures so effectively their shared attitudes toward the brothel subject and its treatment in modern art, that it is worth quoting in full.

"There are suspect parlors by him, of which one in particular wins you over and fascinates you.

In a room with crimson hangings, a gentleman is sitting on a divan, his chin resting on the knob of his umbrella. Standing before him, half-opening their négligées to show their bellies, women try to make him decide: a stout brunette with over-ripe, flecked flesh, resigned to failure; a tall, black-haired woman, the beautiful Jewess, who looks on indifferently, without singing her own praises; a knock-kneed blonde slipping in from behind in her apple-green stockings with red stripes; a cleaned-up street-walker who is laughing and, in the absence of a brief adventure, is preparing to solicit some champagne. Vain efforts, wasted trouble! — the gentleman will not go upstairs or pay for more drinks. If he is incapable of thumping out a polka on the piano, he will be asked politely to take French leave.

What is phenomenal in this work is the powerful reality emanating from it. These whores are brothel whores and no other kind, and if their bodily attitudes, their provocative odor, their gamey skin, under the gas flames that light up this watercolor reworked in gouache with a truly strange realistic precision, are no doubt for the first time rendered so solidly and so bluntly, their character, their bestial or puerile humanity, is no less marked. The entire philosophy of commercial love is in this scene...."[2]

Wonderfully vivid and evocative though it is, Huysmans's text ignores one aspect of *The Client* that Forain evidently had in mind: its witty allusion to traditional representations of The Judgement of Paris.[3] Given Forain's admiration for the old masters whom he copied in the Louvre as an adolescent and continued to study and revere all his life, he was surely aware of the treatments of this familiar theme by Titian, Rubens, and other artists down to his own day. Following the typical compositional schema of a Judgement of Paris, he has shown a seated male figure at one side, gravely considering his choice, and arrayed before him a trio of more or less naked female figures, whose beauty he judges; the other two women are distinctly subordinated, reinforcing the traditional idea of a trio. Moreover, the mythological shepherd's name was perhaps conflated in Forain's mind with his adopted city's name and the site of this brothel scene.

Far from being an unusual personal invention, however, this clever play on the mythological connotation of a modern urban subject was popular in French art and literature at the time. For Forain, perhaps the most relevant examples are two drawings published in the early 1880s in journals to which he too contributed, *La Vie Parisienne* and *Le Courrier Français*. In the first, entitled "JUGEMENT DE la vie PARISienne," a fashion contest among three elegantly dressed society ladies is decided by another lady seated before them, holding <u>three</u> apples.[4] The second, entitled "Le Choix du modèle," shows another kind of beauty contest, in which an artist chooses among three models, whose attitudes and attire are contrasted as clearly as those of the goddesses in a Judgement of Paris.[5]

Theodore Reff

Provenance
Marquis de Biron, Paris; Nicolas Rauch, Geneva, June 13-15, 1960; Reid and Lefevre, London; Roger Alasdair, London; Reid and Lefevre, London; Samuel Basil, London; Hazlitt, Gooden & Fox, London; Galerie Hopkins-Thomas, Paris.

Notes
[1]Lillian Browse, *Forain the Painter, 1852-1931*, London, 1948.
[2]Joris-Karl Huysmans, "L'exposition des Indépendants en 1880," *L'art moderne*, Paris, 1883, pp. 107-108.
[3]Browse has observed (*Forain the Painter*, p. 23) that "when mythology was *à la mode*," *Le Client* "might well have been called *The Judgement of Paris*."
[4]*La Vie Parisienne*, vol. 19, May 28, 1881, p. 314.
[5]*Le Courrier Français*, vol. 1, no. 7, December 28, 1884, p. 1.

45

2.

Parisian Salon
(Salon parisien)

Gouache, watercolor and pencil on wove rag paper
16 1/4 x 13 in. (41.4 x 33 cm.)
Dedicated, signed and dated u.l.: *a mon ami
Huysmans / L. Forain / Août 78* (August 1878)
1878

Parisian Salon plunges us into the genteel atmosphere of social gatherings among the upper bourgeoisie of the Third Republic.[1]

The watercolor and gouache, applied with fluid strokes, provide a vivid evocation of the frivolous elegance of such social events. Forain uses a hatching technique typical of his early works; the lines are widely spaced and he avoids covering the entire sheet with color. Moreover, he plays with the whiteness of the paper, allowing it to show through for a lightened effect. He further heightens this impression by contrasting the men's dark coats with the white of the central lady's dress and of the men's shirt fronts.

The spontaneity of this scene gives the impression of rapid execution by the artist. However, it already reveals the young Forain's sophisticated sense of composition, with its eight figures arranged in a semicircle. The composition draws our attention to the center of the semicircle, where two young lovers are looking intently into each other's eyes. The central couple is also highlighted by the bright colors surrounding them - the red and yellow of the wall, the green of the chair - while the figures on the edge of the semicircle are dark.

Forain gives us his "impression" of society gatherings, observing in detail the poses of the various characters, be they the tilting heads of the two standing men, the withdrawn position of the observer in the red dress or the stiff posture of the figures in the foreground who look bored, in contrast to the intimacy of the two fond lovebirds whose knees are almost touching. He gives us his observation of the "Beau Monde," but makes no attempt at satire.

The faces, those of the women in particular, are typical of Forain around 1878. The round eyes and upturned noses convey no individual character as yet and are barely distinguishable from each other.

Forain must have been satisfied with this work on paper, as he gave it to Huysmans, a friend he greatly esteemed.[2]

It is particularly interesting to note the date of the work, August 1878. It proves conclusively that by age 26 Forain was already admitted to high-society salons. Unlike Manet and Degas who were both from wealthy families, Forain was an artisan's son, the Gavroche of Verlaine and Rimbaud, a mere penniless artist. Yet he managed to open the doors into Parisian society and succeeded in penetrating this privileged world where so many others failed.

Forain's caustic wit and racy conversation enabled him to frequent this social class to which he did not belong. With his lively social intelligence, Forain adapted rapidly to this world and was thus able to describe it freely.

Florence Valdès-Forain

Provenance
J.-K. Huysmans, Paris; Lucien Descaves, Paris; Sotheby's London, November 30, 1988, lot no. 424; Galerie Hopkins-Thomas, Paris.

Notes
[1] The Third Republic was declared in 1870, following the fall of Napoleon III.
[2] On Forain's friendship with Huysmans, see note 46 in the essay "A Portrait of Jean-Louis Forain" in this catalogue and *Frontispiece Refused for Martha* (cat. no. 46).

3.

Parisian Soirée
(Soirée parisienne)

Watercolor, gouache, pencil, India ink on
wove paper
10 1/4 x 12 9/16 in. (26 x 32 cm.)
Signed u.r.: *Louis Forain*
c. 1878

Here, Forain portrays the guests' arrival at a high-society soirée. The main character, in the center of the composition, is a beautiful young woman wearing a white gown whose flounces and blue trimming are represented in detail. She is accompanied by a man who, with his Legion of Honor ribbon and his long side-whiskers, displays every outward sign of respectability. This first couple is followed by another, then a third, while further arriving guests are suggested in the background.

Forain has produced a realistic composition which gives us, the spectators, the impression that we ourselves form part of the scene. To achieve this effect, the artist detaches the foreground figure, whose back is turned to us. As in a photograph, part of his body is cut off by the edges of the picture. Thanks to this method, we feel we are standing next to this character, watching the procession. The effect is further strengthened by the man with sideburns, who is looking towards the spectator.

In fact, Forain has built up a complex criss-crossing of visual exchanges which breathes life into the scene. The pretty young woman is glancing at the person whose back is turned, while a second guest, behind her, gives her a long look as she adjusts her gown. As for her partner, he is turning towards her to exchange a few words.

Forain portrays the atmosphere of high-society events in several contemporary works (*Parisian Salon,* cat. no. 2). Here, he is showing an everyday scene of bourgeois life with no attempt at caricature and a limited narrative content. The title, which is not the original one, does not specify the type of event. The guests are perhaps making their way to the dining room of a sumptuous residence after the butler has solemnly pronounced "Dinner is served."

Maybe the ball is about to commence, or perhaps the figures are lined up for a wedding procession. In any case, it is a friendly observation of courteous attitudes and elegant gowns that Forain gives us in this delicious watercolor. The work is worthy of the most respectable high-society painters of his time, though Forain's techniques are decidedly modern. For example, notice the indigo glints in the hair and whiskers of the third man. They alone would be sufficient to antagonize critics hostile to the Independents.

What surprises one here is the incredible freshness of this watercolor, dominated by acid green and Prussian blue. These cold colors are used pure, and the lavish amounts of red Forain usually applied to his decors at that time only partly restore warmth to the atmosphere.[1] He sketches the scene in pencil. Then as an experienced watercolor artist, he applies his wash with touches of juxtaposed color. As they dry, he obtains patches of varied hue. The bouquet, the console and the floor are flooded with a particularly successful transparency.

Through this work, the artist demonstrates his particular talent for the watercolor technique. Its rapidity of execution prohibited subsequent correction and suited his temperament well. This form of expression, popular among his predecessors, Guys and Lamy, was no longer in fashion and had been abandoned by official painters. As Huysmans remarked in his critique of the Sixth "Impressionist" exhibition in 1881, "Never, never will the public accept Mr. Forain as a painter, solely because he uses watercolor, gouache and pastel and rarely turns to oils. Indeed, one of the ineradicable prejudices of the world is that only oil painting, taught at the Ecole des Beaux-Arts, can be considered as a higher art form..."[2]

FVF

Provenance
Private collection, Paris; Galerie Hopkins-Thomas, Paris.

Notes
[1]For example, *The Client* (cat. no. 1) and *At the Café* (cat. no. 7).
[2]J-K Huysmans, *L'Exposition des Indépendants en 1881,* quoted in *L'Art Moderne,* Paris, 1986, p. 221. *L'Art Moderne* was first published in 1883. Also see note 46 in "A Portrait of Jean-Louis Forain" in this catalogue.

4.

The Anxious Lover

(L'Amoureux transi)

Watercolor on wove rag paper
10 9/16 x 6 5/8 in. (26.8 x 16.8 cm.)
Signed l.r.: *Louis Forain*
c. 1877

This watercolor, characterized by its light and rapid execution, captures the look exchanged between two lovers. Will the young man succeed in expressing the compliments he has prepared for his beloved? His beard seems to hide a childlike face which reflects the character's awkwardness. Everything in his attitude expresses the timidity of youth.

The black coat and elegant gown seem to indicate that the scene is taking place in the "Beau Monde." Moreover, the young woman, with her high chignon and swirling sheath decorated with a garland of flowers recalls the main character in *Parisian Soirée* (cat. no. 3).

FVF

Provenance
Galerie Brame et Laurenceau, Paris; Hazlitt, Gooden & Fox, London; Galerie Hopkins-Thomas, Paris.

Louis Forain

5.

Young Woman Seated
(Jeune femme assise)

Watercolor and gouache on laid paper
10 3/8 x 7 11/16 in. (26.3 x 19.2 cm.)
Unsigned
c. 1877

With a few watercolor strokes, the young
Forain depicts the static pose of a young
woman sitting on a bench in a woody glade.
Centered in the middle of the page, directly
facing us, her face is quite expressionless,
resembling that of a round-eyed doll. In the
same naive spirit, Forain painted *Young
Woman with a Child in a Garden* (fig. no. 1).

FVF

Fig. no. 1. J.L. Forain, *Young Woman with a Child in a
Garden*. Cabinet des dessins of Musée du Louvre, Paris
(RF 29419). ©Photo R.M.N.

Provenance
Jane Roberts, Paris; Galerie Hopkins-Thomas, Paris.

53

6.

The Beautiful Véronique
(La Belle Véronique)

Watercolor, pen and ink
15 13/16 x 10 7/16 in. (40.3 x 26.5 cm.)
Dedicated and signed l.l.: *A Monsieur Théodore de Banville / son admirateur devoué / Louis Forain*
c. 1877
Illustration of the poem "La Belle Véronique" by Banville copied by Forain on right:

> *"It was a gay supper full of surprises*
> *The roasts, perfectly cooked, arrived*
>   *hot and steaming*
> *On this beautiful winter night, cherries*
>   *were on offer*
> *And Johannisberg wine fit for a royal table*
>
> *All these joyful, drunken friends, proud*
>   *of their vices*
> *Exchanged jesting words like a beating*
>   *tambourine*
> *The ladies, however, nibbled on shrimp*
> *And rinsed their fingers in the German wine."*

On verso: sketch of a man in top hat in profile (ink).

Introduced into the poets' circle by Rimbaud and Verlaine,[1] Forain made the acquaintance of Théodore de Banville (1823-1891), to whom he dedicated this charming watercolor. Indeed, it is probably under the influence of his friends that Forain composed his own poems, two of which were published in 1873.[2]

As a "devoted admirer," the young artist appreciated the erudite poems of Banville, a member of the Parnassian poetic movement. He copied out the first two verses of "La Belle Véronique," but, curiously, abandoned the third verse, though it is this very verse which contains the theme he used to illustrate Banville's text:

> *"After putting down his glass, still wet*
>   *with wine,*
> *A young man, his head full of fabulous*
>   *dreams,*
> *Beautiful as Antinoüs, though shy at*
>   *heart,*
> *Beseeched, in a quiet corner his blue-*
>   *eyed neighbour"*

Forain focuses on man's devotion to womankind. He represents a young man throwing himself at the feet of his beloved who is reclining on a sofa. The painter uses the watercolor's transparency to accompany this light-hearted scene.

FVF

Provenance
Collection of Théodore de Banville, Paris; Galerie Hopkins-Thomas, Paris.

Notes
[1] On Forain's friendship with Rimbaud and Verlaine, see the commentary on *On the Verses of Verlaine, a Rogue takes a Stroll in the Country* (cat. no. 43).
[2] The poems signed Louis Forain entitled "*La Danse des pantins*" and "*Dames de comptoir*" appeared on August 31 and November 23, 1873, in a literary journal called *La Renaissance littéraire et artistique* with which Banville was involved.

La Belle Veronique

7.

At the Café

(Au Café)

Gouache and watercolor on paper
12 7/8 x 10 in. (33.3 x 25.8 cm.)
Signed l.r.: *Louis Forain*
c. 1879

Presented at the Fourth "Impressionist" exhibition in 1879, this gouache documents Forain's interest in depicting daily life, particularly scenes in the cafés and "café-concerts" so often chosen by Degas and Manet since 1877-1878.

The young Forain successfully assimilated his masters' teachings, as shown by his careful rendering of the light on the shiny top hats, the men's topcoats and the young woman's jacket. The room is bathed in a milky light, typical of the gas lighting used before the arrival of electricity. It exaggerates the whiteness of the tables and the pallor of the women's complexions. The unseen light source is on the right, producing a dark and clearcut shadow under the hats.

The artist uses a bright range of colors playing with the contrast between red and blue o the one hand and subtle grey and white mono-chromes on the other. He, nevertheless, tones down the color of the red wall by criss-crossing blue brush strokes characteristic of his early works.[1] Two orange touches in the foreground suggest the beer glasses, in the same way as Manet in *Café-concert* (fig. no. 2).

Forain owes his taste for off-center images to Degas, who was influenced by Japanese prints. The three characters sitting in the foreground are truncated at the waist while two figures on the right are cut off by the edge of the canvas. This type of presentation makes the situation more immediate for the spectator. The scene's spontaneity is heightened by the sardonic look from the man sitting at the extreme left.

The scene includes a dozen figures in various poses that are all contained in four rectangles. The general composition is relatively simple compared to that of the *Café-concert* produced by Manet at the height of his career. The atmosphere in the two pictures also differs. In Manet's work, the characters are distant from each other and face in opposite directions. Forain, on

Fig. no. 2. Edouard Manet, *Café-concert*, 1878. Oil on canvas. The Walters Art Gallery, Baltimore, Maryland.

the other hand, depicts characters who are talking in groups of two or three and whose conversations are interrupted by the young woman's arrival.

This woman is clearly the main character. Placed in the center of the composition, she is wearing a colored gown that contrasts with the men's dark coats. She has dared to enter a café alone at night. Forain leaves little room for doubt; she is surely a loose woman, whose silhouette is strangely similar to that of *Walker with an Umbrella* (fig. no. 3).

Forain is interested in observing the effect of this woman on men. She can feel the men's eyes upon her but does not yet speak to them, nor even glance in their direction. She appears aloof, staring far into the distance. Indeed, Forain frequently observes the attitude of women attempting to avoid a man's gaze.[2] Mutinous yet naive, she represents the typical "Parisian" woman.

The three standing male characters have caricatural faces; Forain, the humorist, cannot resist the temptation to add a touch of satire to his works. This satirical edge sets Forain apart from the other Impressionists and in 1879, the critic Diego Martelli remarked: "Forain, a very young man, follows Degas with one foot and the caricaturist Grévin with the other."[3]

FVF

Fig. no. 3. J.L. Forain, *Walker with an Umbrella*. Etching. Boston Public Library, Boston, Massachusetts.

Provenance
Palais Galliera, 1972; Lefevre Gallery, London; Private collection, Switzerland; E.J. van Wisselingh and Co., Naarden, The Netherlands; Private collection, The Netherlands; Galerie Hopkins-Thomas, Paris.

Notes
[1] *Parisian Salon* (cat. no. 2), *Evening at the Opera* (cat. no. 38), *The Client* (cat. no.1).
[2] *Intermission. On Stage* (cat. no. 8).
[3] *Roma Artistica*, June 27 and July 5, 1879.

Cat. no. 7 (Detail)

8.

Intermission. On Stage
(Entracte. Sur la scène)
Watercolor, gouache and India ink, pencil (traces) on wove rag paper
13 7/8 x 10 11/16 in. (35.3 x 27.2 cm.)
Signed and dated l.l.: *L. / Forain / 2 février 1879*
(February 2, 1879)
1879

The curtain has just come down and the ballerinas are going back into the wings, where the static silhouette of the duty fireman can be seen in the background. Still grouped together, they are already being joined by their "protectors."

Forain concentrates on the dancer in the foreground, towards whom an admirer aims his lustful gaze. He exaggerates the character of the the man with the pince-nez who exhibits the red ribbon of his Legion of Honor decoration in his buttonhole, very much like Aristide Saccard,

hero of Zola's novel *La Curée*: "the most clearly visible aspect of his entire person was the red splash of his Legion of Honor ribbon."[1]

The ballerina does not seem to notice her admirer. The pearly hue of her skin, accentuated by the gas lighting, is highlighted by the black ribbon around her neck. However, she is a dancer without charm: her stooped position, her flattened breasts, her drooping shoulders and unattractive face contrast starkly with the graceful beauty of the majority of Forain's dancers. Her arms, thin and long, are partially drawn, as is the chair where she rests the slipper she is retying.

Forain illuminates this derisory spectacle with the bright green of the tutus and the multicolored backdrop. The décor's floral motifs are almost indistinguishable as they are painted with a flickering touch. Like Degas's *Dancers Backstage* (fig. no. 4), Forain plays on the contrast between an abstract representation of the set and a very detailed depiction of the figures. He achieves a similar effect of contrast by placing the black mass of the male figure in front of the colored scenery while the dancers in their colorful, evanescent costumes are grouped together on the far side.

Like many of Degas's works and the Japanese engravings which inspired him, the composition has an abrupt vertical dividing line. The edge of the scenery creates a frontier between the stage and the wings, cutting the space in the same way as the pillar in the foreground of Degas's contemporary etching entitled *Mary Cassatt in the Painting Gallery of the Louvre* (fig. no. 5).

Under Degas's influence, Forain regularly attended the ballet at the Paris Opera House, not only to study feminine anatomy in movement,[2] but also to observe the world of opera-goers, who formed a representative slice of contemporary Parisian society. Though Degas also depicted the Opera-going elite and their protégés at the end of the 1870s,[3] their presence is much less ubiquitous than in the works of Forain.

It would be an oversimplification to say that Forain was interested solely in what the dancers were thinking and Degas solely in their movements and poses: Degas the painter of dancers on stage and at rehearsal, Forain the

Fig. no. 4. Edgar Degas. *Dancers Backstage,* c. 1872. Canvas. Ailsa Mellon Bruce Collection 1970, National Gallery of Art, Washington, D.C.

L. Forain
2 février 79

painter in the wings. However, it is true that Forain, with his essentially humoristic temperament, is a moralistic painter, showing pity for the unfortunate young dancers forced into prostitution for survival.

A vein of satire clearly underlies this observation of reality. The overly-conventional masculine figure with his theatrical expression strongly suggests the anecdotal element. The gentleman's fixed stare towards the young girl's bare breasts takes up the theme of voyeurism, traditional to western art. Though this watercolor is not an exact representation of *Suzanne in the Bath*, it, nevertheless, has similar moralizing intentions. Forain, not content simply to provide an ironic commentary on love, is denouncing its vices. This moralizing temperament sets him apart from other Impressionist painters.

This watercolor was included in the famous "Peau de l'Ours" sale which brought together, just before World War I, works by the new generation of artists such as Picasso, Bonnard, Van Dongen, and Matisse.

FVF

Fig. no. 5. Edgar Degas. *Mary Cassatt in the Painting Gallery of the Louvre*, c. 1879. Etching, aquatint, drypoint and crayon électrique. The Art Institute of Chicago, Illinois, Gift of Walter S. Brewster (1951.323).

Provenance
Collection de "La Peau de l'Ours," Hotel Drouot, Paris, March, 2, 1914, no. 97 of catalogue, illustrated; Emile Level (member of the Peau de l'Ours, brother of André Level); Private collection, Paris; Galerie Hopkins-Thomas, Paris.

Notes
[1]Emile Zola, *La Curée*, Paris, 1990, p. 336.
[2]*Dancer* (cat. no. 40) or *Dancer in a Colored Tutu* (cat. no. 42).
[3]For example, those depicted in the Cardinal Family Monotype series.

Cat. no. 8 (Detail)

9.
At the Theater, Orchestra Seats
(Au Théatre, fauteuils d'orchestre)
Watercolor, gouache, black chalk on wove paper
10 1/8 x 12 3/16 in. (25.7 x 30.8 cm.)
Signed l.l.: *jl. forain*
c. 1880

Forain provides a snapshot of contemporary life moments before the curtain rises, as spectators settle into their seats and talk with their neighbors. He depicts the way people behave, sit and lean towards their neighbors. Though Daumier and Gavarni introduced this vision of everyday life in the 1840s, it still shocked Forain's contemporaries forty years later.

To add a "true to life" touch, the artist details quirky fashion accessories such as ladies' hats and muffs.

He represents the viewpoint of a spectator standing with his back to the stage and facing the sloping stalls. The boxes in the background are merely sketched in pencil. Five spectators are depicted in detail, while others are suggested. Like Daumier *(Les Fauteuils d'orchestre*, fig. no. 6), Forain knows that a few figures are sufficient to represent a crowd.

Forain uses a very light touch to depict the feverish atmosphere of the audience as it waits for the performance to begin. He plays with the paper medium, leaving his figures to float on the white page. Like many of his contemporary watercolors, the color range is both limited and bright with reds and blues.

FVF

Fig. no. 6. Honoré Daumier. *Les Fauteuils d'orchestre*, 1878. Wood engraving. National Gallery of Art, Washington, D.C., Rosenwald Collection (1943.3.5575).

Provenance
Ducousso, Gestas et Bichambre, Pau, France, March 1990; Galerie Hopkins-Thomas, Paris.

64

10.

After the Ball, the Reveler

(Aprés le bal, le noceur)

Pastel on paper
12 1/4 x 18 1/2 in. (31 x 47 cm.)
Signed and dated l.l.: *forain / 81--*
1881

Forain offers an image of debauchery. After a
night of revelry, a dandy lies collapsed in
drunken sleep. The inertness of his body is
particularly well-portrayed by his lifeless, hanging left arm. The Naturalistic artist spares no
detail in his expression of moral decay.

The spectator's plunging viewpoint
draws attention to the shoes, still on the feet of
their wearer, who has clearly been unable to
find the strength either to remove them or to
draw back his bedsheet. The snorer's half-open
mouth adds a crude, yet intimate, note to his
turpitudes.

Dead-drunk, the man is depicted with
the striking foreshortened perspective used by
the great masters for their recumbents,
Mantegna's *Dead Christ,* for example. There is
also a closer reference to Daumier and his
famous *Rue Transnonain* (fig. no. 7).

Forain enjoys playing with the medium
to give an impression of transparency, lightness,
or even spontaneity. He sketches the broad
outlines with charcoal then refines the expression of the face, the folds of clothing and the
crumpled sheets. He then applies broad flat
planes of pastel, though making sure not to
cover the entire surface. The hands are barely
sketched in, merely suggested by a touch of
chalk.

FVF

Fig. no. 7. Honoré Daumier. *Rue Transnonain, le 15
avril 1834,* 1834. Lithograph. National Gallery of Art,
Washington, D.C., Rosenwald Collection (1943.3.2957).

Provenance
Andre Weil; Hazlitt Gallery, London; Lord Goodman, London;
Galerie Hopkins-Thomas, Paris.

11.

In Front of the Stock Exchange No. 1

(Devant la bourse No. 1)

Oil on panel
13 3/4 x 10 1/2 in. (35.25 x 27 cm.)
Signed l.r.: *j.l. forain*
c. 1880

12.

In Front of the Stock Exchange No. 2

(Devant la bourse No. 2)

Oil on panel
13 3/4 x 10 1/2 in. (35.25 x 27 cm.)
Unsigned
c. 1880

A Naturalist painter, Forain liked to observe contemporary life. He wanted to understand the hidden aspects of society, particularly in the theatrical, horse-racing and financial worlds. Consequently, his works often represent the dramas and intrigues played out in the wings of the opera, the terraces of the racecourse and the corridors of the Stock Exchange.

On these two small wooden panels, Forain depicts two financiers exchanging useful tips. He plays with the irregular surface of the wood, making rapid brush strokes with diluted paste.

These two sketches reveal the artist at work with his broad and confident style. He paints characters directly onto the panel without any preliminary charcoal or pencil sketching and is able to portray two figures with a few simple brush strokes.

One of the sketches highlights the stooping back of a corpulent male figure. He leans on the knob of his cane as he listens to the advice of a man whose face is hidden. The other sketch provides a more detailed view of this second figure.

At the end of the 19th century, the Parisian worlds of finance and art were close neighbors, since the art dealers were grouped around rue Laffitte, just a step away from the business quarter. However, their links were often

Fig. no. 8. Edgar Degas, *Portraits, at the Stock Exchange,* c. 1879. Oil on canvas. Musée d'Orsay, Paris. ©Photo R.M.N.

more than merely geographical, since some bankers also prided themselves on their talents as fine-art collectors. Such was the case of Ernest May, painted at the Stock Exchange by Degas in *Portraits, at the Stock Exchange* (fig. no. 8). Degas presented this picture at the Fourth and Fifth "Impressionist" exhibitions in 1879 and 1880, in which Forain took part. Here, Degas's influence on Forain is striking.

FVF

Provenance
Edwardo Moratilla, Paris; Hazlitt, Godden & Fox, London; Lord Goodman, London; Galerie Hopkins-Thomas, Paris.

11.

12.

13.

The Horsewoman

(La Cavalière)

Gouache, India ink, black chalk (traces) on paper
14 1/4 x 8 1/8 in. (36.2 x 20.6 cm.)
Signed l.r.: *j.l. forain*
c. 1882

Poised side-saddle on her horse, a comely horse-woman looks towards a man whose back is turned to us. The spotless paving stones of the courtyard and the copper ball decorating the stall indicate that the meeting is taking place in the stable yard of a luxurious Parisian residence.

This scene of high-society life is nevertheless enigmatic. The viewer is left to ponder whether this is merely a chance encounter or a lovers' tryst.

The atmosphere itself is strange. Light from a milky sky whitens the paving stones. The small shadow cast by the horse in a fleeting shaft of sunlight indicates that the sun is directly overhead. It must be mid-day.

Forain plays with the contrast between this opaline light and the rich black of the horse's coat, its mistress's dress and the gentleman's costume.

The low-angle view amplifies the horse's power and shrinks the rider's figure. The horse-woman appears stiff as does her admirer. This immobility is accentuated by the careful finish of this gouache, unusual in Forain's work.

Handled in a different manner, *The Horseback Ride* (fig. no. 9) is a small contemporary sketch representing a lady riding side-saddle in a natural context, far from the intrigues of society.

FVF

Provenance
Madame Simone Peyre, Carcassone; Galerie Hopkins-Thomas, Paris.

Fig. no. 9. J.L. Forain. *The Horseback Ride.* Oil on wood panel. Private collection, France.

14.
The Bookmaker
(Le Bookmaker)
Watercolor, ink on paper
10 3/4 x 8 7/8 in. (27.4 x 22.5 cm.)
Signed l. r. and dedicated: *A Monsieur Donnadille /
bien cordialement / jl. forain*
On verso: sketches of five silhouettes (ink)
c. 1885

Forain highlights his characters' outlines with a
continuous line applied after the watercolor has
dried. The extreme fluidity of watercolor contrasts with these clearcut lines.

　　Very early in his career, Forain developed
such expert watercolor techniques that he was
able to attack the paper directly with a water-
soaked brush (*The Anxious Lover*, cat. no. 4 or
The Fashionable Women, cat. no. 22). It is
interesting to compare this work with his study
on the same theme entitled *Bookmaker* (fig. no.
10). The systematically highlighted outlines in
the final work, absent from the study, are a
much more experimental touch.

　　The Bookmaker depicts a scene at the
racecourse, but no horses are shown. Forain
portrays a masculine crowd of gamblers, all
wearing top hats and unremarkable topcoats.
Only two figures stand out: the bookmaker in a
bowler hat and a young woman in a hat decorated with red who is oblivious to the bettors
around her.

　　The dichotomy of the racing world with
its jockeys, trainers and bookmakers, mingling
with owners, society figures and women of the
demi-monde, interests Forain the most. Like his
friends Manet, Degas and Toulouse-Lautrec,
Forain attended the races regularly, but it was
not to see the horses themselves. Indeed, they
are either totally absent or relegated to the
background in his magnificent, contemporary,
large format canvases such as *The Race Track*
(fig. no. 11). Though he seems to have a particular talent for portraying horses as in *The Horse-
woman* (cat. no. 13), he prefers to focus his
attention on their entourage.

　　Like the world of dance, which attracts
Forain more than the show on stage, the world
of racing attracts him more than the actual

Fig. no. 10. J.L. Forain. *Bookmaker.* Watercolor. Sale on
November 24, 1992, Phillips, London, lot. no. 301.

Fig. no. 11. J.L. Forain. *The Race Track*, 1884-85. Oil on
canvas. Museum of Fine Arts, Springfield, Massachusetts.
The James Philip Gray Collection.

horses. The same "High Life" personalities are
both horse-owning members of the highly select
Jockey Club *and* regular opera-goers.

　　This watercolor is dedicated to Mr.
Donnadille, a collector who bought *A Corner of
the Opera*, an India ink drawing which appeared
under no. 40 in the catalogue of the Eighth
"Impressionist" exhibition in 1886.

FVF

Provenance
Private collection, Paris; Galerie Hopkins-Thomas, Paris.

15.

Scene of Society Life - The Casino

(Scène de la vie mondaine - le casino)

Watercolor, India ink, gouache highlights, and collage on bristol board
17 3/4 x 24 1/8 in. (45 x 61.4 cm.)
Signed l.l.: *j.l. forain*
Inscriptions u.r.: *Acropole* and *La Redoute*
1884

Using a gambling theme, Forain constructs six scenes which he combines in a humorous juxtaposition of aces of hearts, spades, clubs, and diamonds. They illustrate what goes on at the Acropole-club, a rendezvous site for night-time entertainment.

In the gambling room, an unfortunate penniless player waits under the surveillance of several policemen. Also, a lucky winner discretely leaves with his takings, symbolized by the pancake ("galette") under his arm.[1]

The club is partly covered by the heart, which has pride of place in this inventive composition, since the heart symbolizes romantic adventure. Amorous escapades were also a feature of the "redoute" organized by the Acropole-club. "Redoute" was an eighteenth century word meaning a dance or ball, still in use at the end of the nineteenth century.[2] Forain inscribes this word on the right-hand edge of the heart. He also depicts a young lady preparing herself with the help of her chamber maid. In the club shape, she is seen with a mincing smile; while in the heart shape at the ball, she casts a meaningful glance at a gentleman nearby. This same gentleman also attracts the attention of three other ladies. The ladies' identities remain a mystery. Perhaps they are society ladies dissipating like Renée,[3] Zola's heroine. In any case, a number are "actresses" who would be all too pleased to accept a supper invitation, according to the explanations added in the published version. Indeed, when Forain issued this work under the title *Fantasy on the Acropole-club* (fig. no. 12),[4] humorous explanations were added next to each scene.

Fig. no. 12. J.L. Forain. *Fantasy on the Acropole-Club, L'Art et la Mode*, November 15, 1884. Bibliothèque Nationale, Paris.

The separate collages are still visible on the original work, indicating that the picture probably, from the start, was meant to be printed.

FVF

Provenance
Hotel Drouot, Paris, May 11, 1912; Sessler's Book Shop, Philadelphia; Frédéric Mulys-Sarfati, Paris; Galerie Hopkins-Thomas, Paris.

Notes
[1] In French slang, the "galette" is a metaphor for wealth. Forain also uses this expression in one of his captions in which a woman sighs as she watches her husband enjoying the company of women: "He must own a real packet (galette) to succeed in finding a mistress with that ugly face of his!" (*La Comédie Parisienne*, 2nd series, p. 169).
[2] On May 18, 1893, Forain published in the *Echo de Paris* a drawing entitled *The Day After a "Redoute."* In 1893, Toulouse-Lautrec also printed a lithography entitled *A "Redoute" at the Moulin Rouge* (Bibliothèque Nationale).
[3] Emile Zola, *La Curée*, Paris, 1990, p. 444.
[4] This illustration was discovered by Theodore Reff.

16.

Leaving the Theater,
Night-Time Scene

(La Sortie de théatre, scène nocturne)

Gouache, watercolor, black pastel on heavy wove
paper
12 3/4 x 1O in. (32.5 x 25.3 cm.)
Dedicated and signed l.r.: *A mon ami Zacharie
Astruc / jean louis forain*
c. 1885

"Mr. Degas, Mr. Forain, and Mr. Raffaëlli are
concerned above all with movement, anecdote
and character" noted the art critic Félix Fénéon[1]
who was quick to identify the various developments of Impressionist art.

This watercolor illustrates the perfect
ease with which Forain is able to portray the
dingy atmosphere of a night-time scene. Two
characters, deep in discussion, stand in front of a
poster of which only the first three letters are
visible: "VIE."

Everything hints at the doubtful dealings
of the two protagonists who blend into the
obscurity of the night. Only the saucy expression
of the prostitute emerges distinctly from the
gloom. The pallid light of a street lamp in the
background lights her face. Leering with an
ape-like expression, she has managed to "hook"
a customer, unlike her counterpart in *Frontispiece for "Paris Sketches"* (fig. no. 13) who is still
waiting for a catch. Forain highlights the red
waistcoat and shiny top hat of the man, who is
shown in profile, hand on hip. They discuss the
young lady's "charms," and the viewer is left to
wonder, will they strike a deal?

The word "VIE" on the poster may refer
to any one of a range of unidentifiable events.
We may imagine, however, that Forain is refer-
ring to *La Vie Moderne,* an illustrated weekly
which published some of his drawings between
1879 and 1881. Mr. Charpentier, its director, was
highly favorable to the Impressionists and
organized painting exhibitions on the journal's
premises. For example, in January 1885, an
exhibition was devoted to Zacharie Astruc (1835-
1907), to whom this work is dedicated. Forain

may have presented his friend with this watercolor during that exhibition. Astruc, who exhibited at the First "Impressionist" exhibition in
1874, was an eclectic personality, who worked
simultaneously as a sculptor, painter, poet, and
journalist. An ardent defender of Impressionism,
he was very close to Manet, who painted his
portrait in 1864.

Forain and Astruc were surely long
acquainted since both took part in the Guerbois
and Nouvelle Athènes meetings.[2] Later, in the
1880s, they worked in neighboring studios at
233 Faubourg Saint Honoré.

FVF

Fig. no. 13. J.L. Forain. *Frontispiece for "Paris Sketches,"*
2nd state, 1880 and 1885. Etching. Boston Public Library,
Boston, Massachussetts. This etching illustrates Huysmans's
novel *Les Croquis parisiens* published in Paris in 1880 and
again in 1885.

Provenance
Zacharie Astruc, Paris; Sotheby's London, February 22, 1989, lot no.
17; Galerie Hopkins-Thomas, Paris.

Notes
[1]Félix Fénéon, "L'impressionisme 1887," quoted in Françoise
Cachin, *Fénéon, Au-delà de l'impressionnisme,* Paris, 1966, p. 83.
First published in *L'émancipation sociale (Narbonne),* April 3,
1887. On Fénéon, see commentary of *Portrait of a Man, Presumed
portrait of Félix Fénéon,* cat. no. 33.
[2]The Café Guerbois and the Café de la Nouvelle Athènes: see
note 13 in "A Portrait of Jean-Louis Forain" in this catalogue.

17.

Woman with a Fan
(Femme à l'éventail)

Pastel on paper
35 x 31 in. (88.9 x 78.7 cm.)
Signed l.r.: *j.l. forain*
c. 1883

This magnificent pastel is an exercise in virtuosity. Here, Forain successfully portrays the intense emotion of a fleeting moment -- the feeling of ecstasy and serenity brought on by the perfume of a flower bouquet.

Forain presented this pastel at the Eighth "Impressionist" exhibition[1] under the suggestive title of *Woman Smelling Flowers.* Never has Forain been closer to the Impressionists than with this pastel, striking in its immediacy. Displaying a modernity dear to Baudelaire, "he draws the eternal from the transient."

What a singular subject indeed, this elegant woman, cut off from the world, forgetful of herself, seeking emotion through her sense of smell! Seen in profile, with lowered eyelid and dilated nostril, she forms a whole with her bouquet. She leans on her arm in a natural pose, holding an open fan.

The pastel technique employed in this work confers a sense of gentleness and refinement as well as a feeling of repressed sensuality. The young woman's complexion and the bouquet of flowers have the same powdery luster, so well rendered by the velvet texture of pastel, but impossible to produce with oil or watercolors. The quality of this work is on a par with the most beautiful intimist pastels by Chardin and other eighteenth century masters.

Degas influenced Forain to use the pastel technique after 1878, especially for portraits, like *Portrait of Huysmans* (fig. no. 24), and around 1885 for intimist scenes exalting femininity, such as *Dancer with a Mirror* (cat. no 19). The liveliness of touch and the immediate transcription of a sensation definitely indicate the teachings of Degas.

The woman's femininity is enhanced by the artist's attention to the details of her attire, such as the turquoise dot suggesting an earring and the black Chantilly lace around her neckline.

The lower part of the bouquet is visible through the fan, decorated partly in red. With areas of pastel smoothly blended, Forain successfully suggests the translucent quality of the stretched silk.

This pastel is carefully structured, with curves and straight lines combined in perfect harmony. The woman's curved back takes up the arch of the fan, while its folds correspond to the angle of the picture hanging on the back wall.

FVF

Provenance
Durand Ruel, Paris, c. 1886; Mme. Lanvin, Paris; Galerie Brame et Lorenceau, Paris; Peter Findlay Gallery, New York; Hirschl and Adler Galleries, Inc., New York; Private collection, Paris.

Note
[1] The last collective exhibition organized by the Impressionists in 1886.

18.

Young Woman with a Hat
(Jeune femme au chapeau)
Pastel with tan/grey wove paper with blue flecks
14 3/4 x 13 3/16 in. (37.5 x 33.5 cm.)
Signed u.r.: *j.l.f.*
c. 1885

This young lady's sophisticated pose seems to
have attracted the painter. Her left forearm is
leaning on the back of a chair whose design
recalls the shapely curves of a woman's body.
Indeed, this seat is the only object in the picture.
Forain depicts the model from waist up, sitting
in front of a plain background with a dreamy,
contemplative expression on her face.

The pastel is smooth and gives an effect
of freshness. Its gay coloring and powdery
texture are more flattering to the complexion
than paint.

FVF

Provenance
Private collection, Paris; Starke Taylor, Dallas; Galerie Hopkins-
Thomas, Paris.

19.

Dancer with a Mirror
(Danseuse au miroir)

Pastel on grey/tan wove paper with blue fibers
12 3/8 x 11 1/8 in. (31.4 x 28.3 cm.)
Signed l.r.: *j.l. forain*
c. 1885

Forain leaves it to the viewer to determine
whether this is a young lady in a ball gown or a
dancer gazing at herself in an attitude of feminine charm.

    To depict the frivolity of this pose, Forain
chooses a soft pink harmony, broken solely by
the lively orange and green touch at the top of
the girl's chignon. This young girl is modelled
in a chalky material, particularly appropriate for
capturing the ephemeral.

    Degas, who took an interest in dancers at
rest after 1878, apparently never painted such
narcissistic poses.

FVF

Provenance
Private collection, France; Galerie du Carrousel, Paris; Galerie
Hopkins-Thomas, Paris.

20.

The Debutante
(La Débutante)

Pastel on four ply rag board
18 7/8 x 11 7/8 in. (48 x 30 cm.)
Dedicated and signed l.r.: *a mon ami Verlet / j.l. forain*
1886

This luminous pastel must have been featured at the Eighth "Impressionist" exhibition in 1886, since it fits the description given by the art critics Paul Adam and Félix Fénéon, both committed supporters of the Impressionist cause:

"In producing a perfect caricature of the bourgeois woman, M. Forain particularly excels. He represents a mother admonishing her daughter before the ball. The mother, in profile, appears lumpy despite the straps of her corset and her light red gown. And the curve of her middle-aged back bulges, ready to split the seams. The girl, forming a tight triangle, is lost in a mist, barely visible among the stiff green gauze. Light filters out from the folded paper lampshade, revealing blue wallpaper - a blue that only a Parisian shopkeeper could find to her taste."[1] "A middle-aged woman in a heavy red dress showers words at the tip of a triangle formed by the young girl in her dingy tulle gown."[2]

Forain sketches the decor and the mother's profile in charcoal before applying chalk. To achieve the misty effect of the young girl's gown, he uses only pastel, smoothly blended with his fingertips.

The girl's outstretched arms aptly express her submissive attitude to her mother's reprimands. The humor of the scene is emphasized by the contrast between the girl's slender figure and the imposing bulk of her mother. Indeed, this older woman recalls a character described by Huysmans, "(...) this portly lady squeezed to bursting point into a dreadful bright blue dress, whose bodice supported the soft layers of an immense triple chin." [3]

The satirical intention of this anecdote is confirmed by the version published in the press[4] with the title "*...But what do you intend to do with yourself?*" (fig. no. 14). The pictorial elements are basically the same, only the scenery in the later version is modified by Forain's addition of a bourgeois masculine presence pictured on the wall.

FVF

Fig. no. 14. J.L. Forain. *"But what do you intend to do with yourself?,"* published in *La Comédie Parisienne,* 2nd series, Paris, 1904, p. 187.

Notes
[1] Paul Adam (1862-1920), see " Peintres impressionnistes" quoted in Denys Riout *Les écrivains devant l'impressionnisme,* Paris, 1989, p. 386. First published in *La Revue contemporaine,* April 1886.
[2] Félix Fénéon, "VIIIème exposition impressionniste," quoted in Françoise Cachin, *Fénéon, Au -delà de l'impressionnisme,* Paris, 1966, p. 61. First published in *La vogue,* June 7 and 15, 1886. On Félix Fénéon, see commentary of *Portrait of a Man, Presumed Portrait of Félix Fénéon,* cat. no. 33.
[3] J.-K. Huysmans, *Un Dilemne,* Paris, 1976, p. 317.
[4] March 4, 1888 in *Le Courrier Français,* then in 1904, in *La Comédie Parisienne,* 2nd series, p. 187.

21.

Woman in a Café
(Femme au café)

Oil on panel
18 x 14 1/2 in. (46 x 37 cm.)
Signed l.r.: *forain*
c. 1885

This woman sitting with her glass inevitably recalls Degas's *Absinthe,* 1875-76 (fig. no. 15) and Manet's *The Plum,* c. 1878 (fig. no. 16). We do not know whether the young Forain saw these pictures in his masters' studios, though he certainly visited the exhibitions where they were displayed.[1]   Around 1885, Forain produced two other variations on the same theme: *Waiting* (fig. no. 17) and The *Absinthe Drinker.*[2]   The same influences are also found in Toulouse-Lautrec's work *Hangover* in 1889.[3]

Fig. no. 16. Edouard Manet. *The Plum,* c. 1878. Oil on canvas. National Gallery of Art, Washington, D.C., collection of Mr. and Mrs. Paul Mellon (1971.85.1)

Fig. no. 15. Edgar Degas. *Absinthe,* 1875-77. Oil on canvas. Musée d' Orsay, Paris.

Forain is not depicting the alcoholism or moral decay suggested by Degas or Lautrec: the woman is sitting upright, her eyes are lively, she is smartly dressed. She does not have the listless gaze of Manet's model; she is looking to the left, seeking company. This ambiguous impression that she is waiting for someone may suggest a prostitute looking for a client.

This work is one of the rare oil paintings produced during Forain's Impressionist period. (At that time, the artist preferred to use pastel,

watercolor or gouache.) His wide, rapid and confident strokes give a strong impression of spontaneity which is reinforced by the incompleteness of certain elements. For example, the woman's left hand and purse are merely suggested by two strokes of black paint.

By contrast, Forain depicts her right hand clutching a pair of gloves and the light on her face in great detail. The subtle blue-grey tones of her dress create a halo of color which is reflected in the glass. Forain plays with the contrast between these cold colors and the red seat, set off by the delicate red touches on the hat and lips, though the brightness is toned down by the neutral wall and table.

FVF

Fig. no. 17. J.L. Forain. *Waiting*. Watercolor over graphite. Fogg Art Museum, Harvard University, Cambridge, Massachusetts, bequest of Grenville L. Winthrop (1943.358).

Provenance
Christie's, London, June, 29, 1976, lot no. 228; E.J. van Wisselingh and Co., Naarden, The Netherlands; Private collection, New York; Museum purchase by the Life Members Society in honor of John and Lucy Buchanan.

Notes
[1]Degas presented *Absinthe* at the Third "Impressionist" exhibition in 1877; *The Plum* was on display at the *La Vie Moderne* Exhibition in 1880 and at the Manet retrospective in 1884.
[2]The *Absinthe Drinker*, J.L. Forain, oil on canvas, Museum of Art, Rhode-Island School of Design, Providence, Rhode Island, anonymous gift (60.024).
[3]Reproduced in *Le Courrier Français* on April 21, 1889.

Cat. no. 21 (Detail)

22.

The Fashionable Women
(Les Elégantes)
Watercolor on wove support
12 x 7 7/8 in. (33.5 x 20 cm.)
Dedicated and signed l.l.: *a mon ami R. Verlet / jl.
forain*
c. 1885

Forain, a painter of Parisian life, is essentially interested in interior scenes. Nevertheless, he does depict some scenes of outdoor life, as demonstrated by this watercolor, probably taken from a notebook.

With his brush soaked in very liquid wash, Forain paints from life a number of figures looking in the same direction. They are probably listening to a concert or watching a performance on the bandstand of a public garden. Green splashes suggest the greenery that surrounds them. With considerable mastery, and without the help of pen or pencil outlines, Forain applies direct touches of wash which he then allows to dry. Here, he has abandoned the hatching technique typical of his early work.

Forain dedicated this watercolor to his friend R. Verlet, who worked in a neighboring studio, as indicated by a letter dated August 26, 1889, signed Raoul Verlet.[1] *The Debutante* (cat. no. 20) is also dedicated to Verlet, probably the sculptor Charles Raoul Verlet.[2]

FVF

Provenance
Galerie J.E. Bellier, Paris; E.J. van Wisselingh and Co., Naarden, The Netherlands; Galerie Hopkins-Thomas, Paris.

Notes
[1] Forain Family Archives.
[2] Charles Raoul Verlet or Raoul Charles Verlet (1858-1923). He took part in the 1880 Salon and those of 1887 and 1889, obtaining gold medals for his sculptures and winning a number of official commissions. He won the Grand Prix in 1900 and entered the Académie des Beaux-Arts in 1910.

à mon ami R. Verlet

J. Gran

91

23.

The Ball

(Le Bal)

Watercolor, black chalk, pastel, pencil, black ink on
heavy wove rag paper.
17 3/8 x 11 1/2 in. (44.2 x 29.1 cm.)
Signed l.r.:   *j.l. forain*
c. 1885

This watercolor depicts an amorous conversation
between an aristocratic couple standing apart at
a social gathering. To express their romantic
chatter, Forain uses the light touch of highly
diluted watercolor to soften the blue and red
tones. This flirtatious encounter in a high-society
setting fits in with the eighteenth century French
tradition of romantic merrymaking in which the
painter jokingly brings the decor into the story.
For example, in *Pilgrimage to the Island of
Cythera*,[1] winged cupids whirl around on the
wall and a bust appears to be observing the
lovers' game of seduction.

 The cherubs painted on the walls, the
eighteenth century statue (or in eighteenth
century taste at least), and the circular molding
on the ceiling of the next room all reflect the
rococo decorative style so popular in late nineteenth century bourgeois interiors.

 Forain's reference to the eighteenth
century is hardly surprising, as Edmond and
Jules de Goncourt brought this aesthetic ideal
back into fashion with their work[2] on eighteenth century art. The title of Verlaine's collection of poems, *Les Fêtes galantes*,[3] is a direct
allusion to the natural decors which provided
the setting for the entertainments of refined
society.   Forain must certainly have been
acquainted with them. He loved poetry, particularly that of his friend Verlaine, whose poem
"L'Ami de la nature"[4] he illustrated.

FVF

Provenance
Private collection, France; Galerie du Carrousel, Paris; Galerie
Hopkins-Thomas, Paris.

Notes
[1] *Pilgrimage to the Island of Cythera*, 1717 by Jean-Antoine Watteau
(1684-1721), Musée du Louvre, Paris.
[2] In 1859.
[3] In 1869.
[4] See *On the Verses of Verlaine, a Rogue Takes a Stroll in the
Country* (cat. no. 43) which illustrates "L'Ami de la nature," a poem
written during the same period as *Les Fêtes galantes*.

24.

The Invitation

(L'Invitation)

Watercolor, ink on paper
11 3/4 x 8 7/8 in. (29.8 x 22.5 cm.)
Dedicated and signed l. r.: *a M. Ferdinand Crouan /
forain*
c. 1890
On verso: sketch of heads of three women (watercolor)

The characters in this romantic scene are portrayed in very similar attitudes to those of *The
Ball* (cat. no. 23) and *Idyll* (fig. no. 18). In the
foreground, an elegant young lady in a low-cut
evening gown turns her head to listen to a
dandy's murmured compliments. She holds a fan
in gloved hands while he carries a top hat and
leans casually, with crossed legs, against a
column or a wall.

 An experienced watercolor artist, Forain
applies a very fluid, almost transparent wash to
suggest the young woman's diaphanous gown.
The masculine forms, with more clearcut outlines, are depicted with energetic brush strokes.

 This wash drawing is dedicated to a Mr.
Fernand Crouan. It is very likely that this is the
same collector, Mr. Crouant who, in 1891, lent
one[1] of the seven works that Forain presented at
the gallery of Georges Petit, the famous art
dealer, for the exhibition of the Société des
Pastellistes Français. Puvis de Chavannes,
Helleu and A. Besnard also took part in this
exhibition.

 FVF

Fig. no. 18. J.L. Forain. *Idyll*. Pen and black ink. Sterling
and Francine Clark Art Institute, Williamstown, Massachusetts.

Provenance
Gabres, Geneva, December 8, 1990; Galerie Hopkins-Thomas, Paris.

Note
[1]*Dancers and Opera-goers,* no. 76 in the *Catalogue of the Société
des Pasteillistes Français.*

à mi Fernand Oroua
forain

25.

Conversation
(Conversation)
Watercolor on wove heavy card
18 3/4 x 13 1/8 in. (47.7 x 33.4 cm.)
Signed l.r.: *f*
c. 1885-1890

In this light sketch, Forain plays with the effect
of the dancer's white tutu which blends into the
white paper.

FVF

Provenance
Galerie Fisher-Kiener, Paris; Galerie Hopkins-Thomas, Paris.

26.

The Conversation, Talking Late into the Night
(La Conversation, discussion tardive)

Watercolor, ink and pen on wove paper, originally
blue-flecked, faded
8 11/16 x 6 5/16 in. (22 x 16 cm.)
Unsigned
c. 1890

With a pencil and a pen, Forain suggests a
conversation between a high-society couple. The
man, facing us, is holding a cup of coffee while
the woman, with back turned, fans herself.

    The woman's low-cut gown and the
man's evening dress indicate that the setting
must indeed be a fashionable soirée. The man's
costume is merely suggested by his white shirt
front, since he blends into the black wash that
Forain uses to cover the left side of his picture.
This exceptionally uniform wash produces an
abrupt and even shadow, contrasting with the
untouched paper on the right-hand side. It also
contrasts with the four crude patches of color on
the woman's figure: yellow for her chignon,
white for her gaslight-flooded skin, green for her
dress, and red for the divan.

FVF

Provenance
Galerie Brame et Lorenceau, Paris; E.J. van Wisselingh and Co.,
Naarden, The Netherlands; Galerie Hopkins-Thomas, Paris.

27.

Monte Carlo

(Monte Carlo)

Watercolor, black crayon or chalk on wove paper
11 5/16 x 8 1/4 in. (28.7 x 21 cm.)
Signed l.r.: *forain*
Dated u.r.: *monte-carlo / 6-mars-1893*
(March 6, 1893)
1893

A few weeks before sailing to America for a six-month trip, Forain stayed on the Riviera.

With a few brief strokes, he sketches a leisured upper-class couple typical of casino-going society. The woman's severe and haughty profile seems to be reprimanding her companion. The drooping shoulders and disenchanted look of the man with his carelessly poised monocle say much about his phlegmatic nature. We can imagine that Madame is reproaching him for his excessive gambling habits.

FVF

Provenance
Private collection, Paris; Galerie Hopkins-Thomas, Paris.

28.

The Visit
(La Visite)

Watercolor with pencil and gouache on wove paper
11 3/4 x 8 7/8 in. (29.8 x 22.5 cm.)
signed l.r.: *j.l. / forain*
c. 1889

In this muted watercolor, Forain denounces the way in which simple young girls are exploited by their families and encouraged into a life of vice. The corresponding drawing which appeared in the press (fig. no. 19) carries the caption: "Oh, your Excellency, you spoiled our little Nini for so long that she's missed her dancing lesson again."

The portly figure of the old gentleman is matched by the equally imposing figure of the mother, who is pleading for compensation to make up for the missed dancing lessons. Still in her chemise, the young girl stands in the back, leaving her mother to negotiate while she brushes her hair.

In Forain's social satire, it is the mothers who, with business-like efficiency, sell the young girls into the night: "Your Excellency, you're all the same with your flowers... they cost just as much as a little something, for only half the effect...."[1]

These mothers have the obliging attitude of Madame Cardinal in Ludovic Halévy's[2] successful novel, *La Famille Cardinal*, illustrated by Degas. This theme is so frequently exploited by Forain that some of his illustrations bear the title "Mothers." He observes the protective complicity of maternal love but also shows us the kept women who have "made their way in the world" and who now relegate their own mother to the rank of a servant: "Aren't you coming home for dinner?" " No, you can finish the duck in the kitchen."[3]

Forain pities the fate of young girls who are forced to prostitute themselves for survival; however, he becomes ferocious in his depiction of those who so skillfully exploit their charms.

FVF

Fig. no. 19. J.L. Forain. Drawing published in no. 1 of *Le Fifre*, February 22, 1889 and republished in *La Comédie Parisienne*, 1st series, Paris, 1892, p. 81.

Provenance
Stoppenbach et Delester, London; Christies New York, May 7, 1974, lot no. 297; E. Franklin Robbins; Sotheby's Arcade New York, October 12, 1991, lot no. 6; Galerie Hopkins-Thomas, Paris.

Notes
[1]J.L. Forain, *La Comédie Parisienne*, 1st series, 1892, p. 147.
[2]Ludovic Halévy (1834-1908): librettist and novelist, an intimate friend of Degas's until the Dreyfus Affair separated them in 1897.
[3]J.L. Forain, *La Comédie Parisienne*, 2nd series, 1904, p. 33.

29.

Can't Trust an English Accent!
(Fiez vous donc à l'accent anglais!)

Watercolor, gouache, pen and black ink on wove rag paper
14 x 10 7/8 in. (35.5 x 27.7 cm.)
Signed l.r.: *j.l. forain*
Inscription along lower edge: *Fiez vous donc à l'accent anglais!..*
1889

Fig. no. 20. J.L. Forain. *Le Fifre*, May 11, 1889. This satirical drawing is also featured on page 67 of *La Comédie Parisienne*, 1st series, Paris, 1892, an album devoted to Forain's social satire.

Forain depicts a prostitute in a chemise with bared breasts. She is sitting on the edge of a bed, and the presence of the man with whom she has just spent the night is suggested by the crown of his head showing above the bedclothes. She examines her client's boot and notes how worn it is. The gentleman is no foreigner despite the hint of an accent she thought she detected in his voice; he is French and is well aware of the going rates. The night will not be as profitable as she had hoped. Hence her indignant, somewhat anxious remark: "Can't trust an English accent!"

This fluid and lightly colored watercolor was used as an illustration (fig. no. 20) in *Le Fifre,* a weekly journal created in 1889 by Forain. Another illustration in *Le Fifre,* on the same theme of early morning disappointment (fig. no. 21), won admiration from numerous artists such as Rodin, who sent Forain a highly laudatory letter heretofore unpublished: [1]

April 2, 1889
182 rue de l'Université

Dear Mr. Forain,
I am flattered by your kindness in sending me a copy of your journal. I greatly admire this drawing method, which is first of all the right one, and which will gradually replace the old type of illustrations because it is sincere and biting like an analysis.

I find that the young girl looking at the trousers reminds me of the drawings on Etruscan vases. Which proves, in my view, that true modernity lies with talented draftsmen.

Yours truly,

Rodin

Fig. no. 21. J.L. Forain. *Le Fifre*, March 30, 1889.

What attracted Rodin was Forain's modernity, defined, in his words, by a "sincere and biting" realism comparable to that of primitive artists. Rodin refers to the illustration entitled *Love in Paris* featured in no. 6 of *Le Fifre,* dated Saturday March 30, 1889, which he had just received. The night will be less profitable than expected for this young woman who notes the poor quality of the gentleman's trousers, exclaiming: "Some poor fellow's pants."

FVF

Provenance
Galerie Hopkins-Thomas, Paris.

Note
[1]Forain Family Archives.

Frez vous donc a l'attent anglais !...

J. L. Forain

105

30.

Two Figures Back to Back
(Deux personnnages dos à dos)

Pen and ink, colored pencil, crayon on wove paper
16 1/8 x 12 1/8 in. (41 x 30.8 cm.)
Signed l.r.: *forain*
c. 1895

These lovers, surprised in their intimacy, are
typical characters of Forain's social satire. This is
certainly a clandestine rendezvous in a hotel
room, as indicated by the man's hat and the
woman's umbrella, carelessly dropped on the
chair. While the woman brushes her hair, the
lover peers anxiously out of the window looking
to see if they have been followed. This drawing
recalls an illustration in *Le Courrier Français*
entitled *The Joys of Adultery* (fig. no. 22).

FVF

Fig. no. 22. J.L. Forain. *Le Courrier Français*, April 22,
1894. *The Joys of Adultery*, caption: *We shouldn't have
taken our boots off! There's no boot-hook!*

Provenance
M. and Mme. Claude Cueto, Paris; Galerie Hopkins-Thomas,
Paris.

31.
The Secret or *The Confidence*
(Le Secret ou *La Confidence)*
Gouache, watercolor, pencil on wood pulp card
7 3/16 x 5 3/16 in. (18.2 x 13.3 cm.)
Signed l.r.: *forain*
c. 1895

This small sketch represents an attitude of which
Forain was particularly fond: the intimate confidence. Drawn in pencil then highlighted with
watercolor and gouache, this scene is portrayed
by Forain with great ease, in a style that is more
suggestive than descriptive.

    The masculine jacket along with the
feminine gloves and fan suggest that the two
protagonists are attending a soirée. The man
takes his partner to one side to whisper a few
words in her ear. The man's curved back and
the woman's tilted head as she leans on her
arms combine to give the impression of a shared
secret. Forain portrays this scene with great
ease, in a style that is more suggestive than
descriptive.

    A painter of human behavior, Forain
wanted to understand life. However, he was not
satisfied with mere appearances. He sought to
capture the hidden side of life with its subter-
fuges, intrigues and innuendoes. What may
appear to us as apparently confused or incom-
prehensible situations are actually Forain's
interpretations of romantic secrets (*The Confidence*, fig. no. 23), financial affairs (*In Front of
the Stock Exchange*, cat. nos. 11,12) or racing
tips (*The Tip-off*, National Gallery of Art, Washington, D.C.).

FVF

Fig. no. 23. J.L. Forain. *The Confidence*, 1885. Watercolor,
signed l.r. Private collection, France.

Provenance
Galerie Hopkins-Thomas, Paris.

108

32.

The Look
(Le Regard)

India ink (pen and brush), red conti, blue watercolor,
ocher watercolor on wove paper
13 1/8 x 9 1/2 in. (33.4 x 24.2 cm.)
Signed l.r.: *jl forain*
1892

Published on November 15, 1892, in *La Revue
Illustrée,* with the caption "I haven't been stared
at like that in years!" this scene of society life
depicts a woman showing surprise at the admiring look she is receiving. She appears to appreciate the man's insistent gaze, which brings back
to mind the numerous compliments she received
in her youth.

     Forain uses both vigorous brush strokes
and translucent patches in this work. One of the
patches that divides the woman's face may be
accidental in a manner reminiscent of Picasso.

FVF

Provenance
Private collection, Paris; Galerie Hopkins-Thomas, Paris.

111

33.

Portrait of a Man, Presumed Portrait of Félix Fénéon
(Portrait d'un homme, portrait présumé de Félix Fénéon)
Pastel on paper
23 3/8 x 19 in. (59.4 x 48.3 cm.)
Dated and signed l.r.: *forain / 1892*
1892

In the 1880s and 90s, numerous artists, including Manet[1] and Toulouse-Lautrec,[2] were broadly inspired by the Italian renaissance and began portraying figures in profile. This magnificent portrait, along with that of *Young Woman with a Hat* (cat. no. 18), probably belongs to this trend.

Forain depicts his model in profile to emphasize his sharp, angular features. He uses a continuous line to highlight the masculine contours which are further accentuated by the bright, plain turquoise background.

Indeed, plain backgrounds and barely sketched details of clothing are characteristic of Forain's portraits *(Portrait of J.K. Huysmans*, fig. no. 24). Far from being a society painter anxious to represent the social rank of his model, Forain aims to reveal each individual's unique character. Through observation, he seeks both to achieve physical resemblance and to portray temperament. This model is enigmatic with his solemn expression and half-closed eyes. The impression of austerity is reinforced by the plainness of his jacket.

While the background is shaded with rapid vertical lines and the bust by large flat planes of color, Forain uses his pastel stick with great care to depict the face. The artist is a past master in the delicate art of pastel. In particular, notice the transparent quality of the skin, strikingly rendered by superimposed strokes of color. The modeling of the face is powerful, highlighted by the imposing cheekbone and brow. The beard is thick in comparison to the hair.

Fig. no. 24. J.L. Forain. *Portrait of J.-K. Huysmans*, Pastel, circa 1878, Musée d'Orsay, Paris, on loan from the Musée National du Château de Versailles. ©Photo R.M.N.

The model's identity remains undetermined; no dedication or note is found on the picture. Only the date, 1892, is certain.

However, this face suggests that of the famous critic Félix Fénéon (1861-1944). In 1890, Signac represented his profile in an "angular pose,"[3] portraying emaciated features and a mysterious personality comparable to this portrait by Forain. However, in Signac's picture, Fénéon is wearing the famous goatee so characteristic of his

113

physiognomy.[4] For this portrait to be of Fénéon, we would have to accept that Fénéon had a beard and moustache – rather than a goatee – when he posed for Forain.

Fénéon is also identifiable in a drawing published in 1894 by Forain himself (fig. no. 25). This illustration represents the trial of the "thirty" anarchists with Fénéon among the accused.[5] Fénéon, again in profile, is recognizable by his sharp nose, his prominent cheekbones and goatee. When Fénéon edited the Natanson brothers' famous *Revue Blanche,*[6] Forain sketched him again.[7]

We do not know when the two men met, though it was probably in the 1880s. In 1884 Fénéon mentioned Forain among "the painters who are inspired by Manet without copying him" and whom "the public must seek to understand, now that they deign to admire Manet who is with us no longer."[8] Even though his name was more directly associated with the defense of neo-Impressionism, Fénéon commented on some of Forain's works, such as *The Débutante* (cat. no. 20). There is every reason to believe that the "rebel" Forain, close to the anarchist movement as a young man, appreciated the anarchist temperament and humor of this inscrutable man.

In a letter addressed to Forain,[9] Fénéon proudly mentions Forain's portrait of him. Fénéon may be alluding to this pastel. However, if Forain gave it to him, the question of what did Fénéon do with it lingers.[10]

FVF

Fig. no. 25. J.L. Forain. *Anarchist Peril,* reproduced in *Le Figaro,* August 17, 1894 and in Forain's album *Doux Pays,* p. 49 (1897).

Provenance
George Syme, Paris; Galerie Hopkins-Thomas, Paris.

Notes
[1] For example, the portrait of Irma Bruner (*Viennese Lady*) or of Méry Laurent (*Autumn*).
[2] For example, *Countess Alphonse de Toulouse-Lautrec in the Salon of the Château of Maromé* or *Hélène Vary.*
[3] Letter from Signac to Fénéon of July 21, 1890, published by Françoise Cachin in "Le portrait de Fénéon par Signac: une source inédite" (Press cutting, documentation of Musée d'Orsay). Signac's *Portrait of Félix Fénéon,* 1890, oil on canvas, is in a private collection.
[4] Fénéon's personality attracted the attention of numerous artists, such as Vallotton, Toulouse-Lautrec and Luce. He is often represented with his goatee in portraits and caricatures.
[5] A committed anarchist, Fénéon was suspected of taking part in one of the anarchist attacks which shook the whole of France leading up to the assassination of President Carnot in 1894. He was acquitted at the joint trial of the "Thirty" on August 8, 1894.
[6] Fénéon edited *La Revue Blanche* from 1895 to 1903.
[7] The catalogue issued for the sale of Mme. Thadée Natanson's estate includes drawings by Forain representing Fénéon and Barrès on headed notepaper of *La Revue Blanche* (cat. no. 39, not reproduced, sale of November 27, 1954).
[8] *Libre Revue,* April 1884.
[9] Forain Family archives.
[10] This pastel is not included in the four posthumous sales of the Fénéon Collection in 1947.

Cat. no. 33 (Detail)

34.

Bust of Diana
(Diane en buste)

Pastel on linen canvas prepared with gesso
18 1/8 x 15 x 1 in. (46 x 38 x 2.5 cm.)
Signed l.r.: *jl. forain*
c. 1890-1895

In this magnificent half-length portrait, Forain highlights the model's neck, which is lengthened by the low-angle viewpoint. With great mastery, the artist achieves the foreshortening of the face required by his desired angle of observation. Powerfully sketched with charcoal, the young woman's features are then sculpted with vigorous strokes of chalk.

This is an unusual choice of subject for Forain, the realist. Arsène Alexandre, who remembers another effigy of the goddess by Forain, is surprised to see him inspired by a myth of this kind. "We can expect certain specimens of his period of apprenticeship and even of his younger years to turn up in the most surprising places. I remember, for example, that his studio at the famous 233 Faubourg St. Honoré was cluttered by a large, tall canvas, representing Diana rising up into the sky with her crescent moon and arrow. It was a most agreeable work, somewhat reminiscent of Baudry."[1]

After his marriage in 1891, Forain left the Parisian artists' colony of the Faubourg Saint-Honoré.[2] Therefore, the painting remembered by Alexandre must be of an earlier date. The pastel technique used in the picture corresponds to the period 1890-95, and is similar to that of another pastel, probably representing the same model with her accompanying crescent moon (*Portrait of a Woman,* fig. no. 26). The *Bust of Diana* may be a study for the lost canvas, or it was perhaps produced at a later date.

Diana seems to be the only mythical character painted by Forain. His interest in Diana may have been linked to Forain's love of dancing. Indeed, from its first performance in 1876, the heroine in the ballet *Sylvia or the Nymph of Diana* wore a crescent moon in her

hair.[3] Forain, a regular spectator at the opera-ballet, must certainly have seen Delibes's successful production. The 1892 and 1893 performances may have been Forain's source of inspiration for *Bust of Diana.*[4] Perhaps he asked the dancer who played Sylvia to pose for him, or he may have hired a professional model to assume the attitude of Sylvia releasing an arrow.

FVF

Fig. no. 26. J.L. Forain. *Portrait of a Woman.* Pastel. M. and Mme. Maréchaux, Paris.

Provenance
P. and D. Colnaghi and Co., Ltd. London; M. and Mme. F. Spingell, London; Sotheby's London, March 23, 1983, lot no. 105; Galerie Hopkins-Thomas, Paris; Hammer Galleries, New York; Private collection, Great Britain; Hazlitt, Gooden & Fox, London; Galerie Hopkins-Thomas, Paris.

Notes
[1]"Forain as he was," *La Renaissance,* XIVth year, no. 1, January 1931, p. 283. This passage was brought to my attention by Theodore Reff.
[2]The studios at 233 Faubourg Saint Honoré were occupied by many of Forain's friends, such as Toulouse-Lautrec, Z. Astruc (see *Leaving the Theater,* cat. no.16) and R. Verlet (see *The Fashionable Women,* cat. no. 22).
[3]Suggestion by C. Coutin, curator at the Bibliothèque Nationale, Paris.
[4]*Sylvia* was performed five times at the Paris Opera in 1892 and once in 1893.

35.
The Echo of Paris
(L'Echo de Paris)

Watercolor, black crayon on laid paper
12 1/8 x 9 1/8 in. (30.8 x 23.2 cm.)
Signed l.r.: *forain*
c. 1899

Every week in 1892 and 1893 and then from
1899 to 1902, *L' Echo de Paris* featured a drawing by Forain. The watercolor indicates that the
journal possibly commissioned Forain to produce an advertisement, along the lines of the
one produced by Chéret for *Le Courrier
Français* in 1891 (fig. no. 27).

The artist sketches a nymphet presenting
the newspaper. However, the idea appears to
have stopped here, since no trace of a more
complete work appears in *L'Echo de Paris* during
the years in which Forain worked for the journal.

FVF

Fig. no. 27. J. Cheret. *Courrier Français,* poster, reproduced in *L'Echo de Paris* on January 4, 1898, p. 4 and
Le Courrier Français on January 14, 1900.

36.

Two Women on Bicycles
(Deux femmes à vélo)

Gouache, chalk on brown paper
29 3/4 x 61 3/4 in. (76 x 157 cm.)
Signed m.l.: *j.l. forain*
October, 1894

This work is a study for the poster of the "Salon du Cycle" bicycle exhibition. It measured 36 x 82 in. and was reproduced on a smaller scale in 1897 in a publication called *Les Maîtres de l'Affiche* (fig. no. 28).

Following in the footsteps of Chéret, Forain uses the illustrated poster as a new mode of expression, alongside artists of the younger generation such as Toulouse-Lautrec, Vuillard and Bonnard.

Forain and Lautrec introduced sport into the plastic arts. Unlike his young friend (*The Simpson Chain,* fig. no. 29), Forain does not seek to give an impression of speed. The two sportswomen are in a static pose, their cycling activity suggested merely by the handlebars and their sporting outfits. Simplifying and stylizing their forms, he proceeds by large flat planes of restrained color; a far cry from Mucha's sinuosities, his poster displays a surprising economy of style. Both as a poster designer and draftsman, Forain is a master of the art of synthesis and ellipsis.

Cycling became highly popular at the end of the nineteenth century. Ladies only launched themselves into the streets after taking lessons, as automobile drivers were to do later. Forain was a man of his time, interested in all the novelties that appeared, including the bicycle. He was a sporting man, enjoying bicycle and tricycle rides as early as 1890, as indicated by Degas in a letter to Ludovic Halévy:[1]

> *Melun - 9h1/2*
>
> *You don't give Brie like that to Parisians! Forain tells the waiter. He has arrived on his tricycle, in Garibaldian dress, and speaks about the fortunes of the bicycle. He is standing and talking with a piece of cheese in his mouth.*

FVF

Fig. no. 28. J.L. Forain. *The Second Bicycle Exhibition,* poster in four colors, printer: H. Hérold. The Dixon Gallery and Gardens, Memphis, Tennessee.

Fig. no. 29. Toulouse-Lautrec. *The Simpson Chain,* 1896. Lithograph. The Guardsmark, Inc. Collection, Memphis, Tennessee.

Provenance
Private collection, Paris; Galerie Hopkins-Thomas, Paris.

Note
[1]Letter dated October 18, 1890, published in Degas's correspondence by Guérin (1931, p. 175; 1945, p. 173). This reference was suggested by Theodore Reff.

37.

In Front of the Set
(Devant le décor)

Pastel on paper
19 1/2 x 23 3/4 in. (49.5 x 60.5 cm.)
Signed l.r.: *forain*
c. 1895-1900

A feeling of storm in the air adds tension as an opera-goer and a dancer meet under the peaceful seascape of an opera set. The ballerina stares into the distance with her face conveying a look of worry, perhaps, even terror. Her companion's expression is more one of lassitude and disillusionment. The viewer is left to ponder what is occurring.

Forain does not provide the key to the mystery. We are free to imagine as we please the next episode in this comedy of manners. It may be a scene from a Feydeau-style farce in which the husband, the lover, the wife, or the mistress suddenly appears. Or the dancer may be simply listening to her companion's confidences as she waits for her entry on stage.

Forain rarely leaves the spectator in such uncertainty. The narrative content of his genre paintings is often not only explicit, but ironic and moralizing, as in *Intermission. On Stage* (cat. no. 8).

Forain was nicknamed "the Lion of Drawing"[1] and, in this pastel, he has indeed bared his claws. With a few powerful charcoal strokes, he sketches in the dancer's bust and face. With a line of white chalk, he confidently suggests the light on her brow, on the bridge of her nose, on her shoulder, and the folds of her tutu.

The artist handles the pastel differently for the dancer, the opera-goer and the background. To portray the grace of the dancer's body, he uses very little powder and plays with the texture of the paper, tracing diagonal lines on her breast and arms and using broad blurred patches of color for the tutu.

Forain focuses attention on the dancer with her protector relegated to the shadow of a stage curtain. His silhouette, depicted with strong charcoal lines, is brought out solely by the whiteness of his shirt front and the illumination of his profile. In contrast to these two characters, the scenery is depicted with bright, compact colors.

Fig. no. 30. *In the Wings,* gouache on card. Musée du Petit Palais, Paris (N.D. 0855). ©Musée de la Ville de Paris by SPADEM 19.

Because Forain is not seeking to convey an atmosphere of fulfillment, this pastel does not have the velvet texture and softness of *Woman with a Fan* (cat. no. 17), produced some ten years earlier. By the age of forty, Forain's drawing technique developed into a rapid, incisive, elliptic and, above all, highly personal style. The same concise quality is achieved in *In the Wings* (fig. no. 30), a contemporary gouache in which the brush moves nervously across the paper, in a style similar to that of Daumier, who used his brushes like pencils.

FVF

Provenance
Jean Lepetit, Paris; Marc Blondeau, Paris; Galerie Hopkins-Thomas, Paris.

Note
[1]By the writer Marie de Régnier, wife of the famous poet Henri de Régnier. See Robert Fleury, *Marie de Regnier*, Paris, 1990, p. 173.

38.

Evening at the Opera (fan)
(Soirée à l'opera (éventail))
Gouache, some pencil or chalk at left on parchment
6 5/8 x 23 1/4 in. (16.8 x 59 cm.)
Signed l.l.: *Forain*
c. 1879

This fan provides a synthesis of all that Forain most liked about the Opera in the 1880s. Infinitely more interesting to Forain than the performance itself is what is happening behind the curtain, in the wings, and in front of the curtain in the spectators' boxes.

To distinguish between these two worlds, he plays with the contrast between the complementary colors of red and green. Despite the intensity of these two pigments, the transition is gradual, subtly suggested by the progressive use of red hatching. After all, these worlds are not totally separate: the same spectators watch the performance with their elegant ladies and then take up with the young dancers after the show.

Forain also plays with the opposition between rounded forms and vertical lines. The convex shape of the fan, the rounded form of the spectators' boxes and the curves of the tutus contrast with the jutting sets over the wings and the elongated masculine figures.

The edges of the fan are left neutral to avoid an impression of over-abundance, to allow it to "breathe." The rest of the set is bare except for an abandoned slip of paper. The symbol of this lover's note is borrowed from the western tradition of romantic scenes, as are flowers which are often used to represent the opera-goer's devotion to his prima-ballerina (*The Toff with a Bouquet,* cat. no. 45). At the other edge, a high-society lady cools herself with a fan in an amusing reference to the material of the fan.

At the Fourth "Impressionist" exhibition in 1879, Forain presented several untitled fans. *Evening at the Opera* may well have figured among them.

FVF

Provenance
Sotheby's London, December 2, 1987, lot no. 453; Galerie Hopkins-Thomas, Paris; David Ramus, Atlanta; Donna Neuhof, Dallas; William Beadleston, New York; Galerie Hopkins-Thomas, Paris.

Cat. no. 38 (Detail)

39.

Ballet in the Garden (fan)

(Ballet dans un jardin (éventail))

Watercolor, pencil on wove paper
7 1/2 x 23 3/4 in. (19 x 60. 4 cm.)
Dedicated and signed l.l.: *a Madame Ducasse /*
Hommage de / j.l. forain 23 juin 1886 (June 23, 1886)
1886

In this watercolor Forain explores the possibilities
provided by a curved format. The arched shape of
the screen is matched by the exaggerated round-
ness of the dancer's tutu and the artificially curved
backdrop. To break this balance of curves, Forain
includes a number of straight lines, such as the
column in the foreground which creates a volume.
Similarly, the stage flat forms a second projecting
element, contrasting with the plane of the picture
and with the gardens in deep perspective.

In this fan, Forain does not seek to achieve
the asymmetrical[1] effect of which Degas was so
fond. Notice the lower right where Forain adds a
truncated pillar surmounted with a bouquet, sym-
metrical to the lower left column.

Dated June 23, 1886, this fan represents a
love duet symbolized by two winged cherubs.
Though these cupids are the fruit of the artist's
imagination, this charming composition probably
takes its inspiration from the opera *Henry VIII*
which was performed five times in 1886. Indeed,
the opera's libretto specifies that "the second act
takes place in Richmond Gardens, in front of a
square of greenery from which several avenues
lead." This opera by Camille Saint-Saëns also
included a choreographic interlude,[2] and the
ballerina's performance received warm praise from
a critic, "Miss Julia, light as a butterfly and mischievous as a fairy."[3]

In *Le Courrier Français* of January 20, 1889,
Forain also reproduced a fan entitled *Scene at the*
Opera (fig. no. 31), whose poses and scenery recall
those of *Ballet in the Garden*. *Henry VIII* had been
performed several times before this illustration
appeared.[4]

A sketch (fig. no. 32) shows that the artist
considered representing a nighttime scene and
using gold dust like Degas had in some of his fans
(*Fan: The Ballet*, fig. no. 33).

Fig. no. 31. J.L. Forain. *Scene at the Opera*, published in *Le Courrier Français,* January 20, 1889.

Fig. no. 32. J.L. Forain. *Fan, sketch*. Gouache on paper. Private collection.

Provenance
Private collection, Paris; Galerie Hopkins-Thomas, Paris.

Notes
[1]See commentary on the *Dancer* fan (cat. no. 40).
[2]In a choreographic interlude, the costumes may be anachronis-
tic with respect to the main opera. On this fan, the male costume
is taken from the eighteenth century.
[3]Stoulig and Noël, *Annales du Théâtre et de la Musique, Opéra*
1885/97, n.p.
[4]In 1888, *Henry VIII* was performed three times.

FVF

Cat. no. 39 (Detail)

40.

Dancer (Fan)
(Danseuse (éventail))

Crayon, graphite, watercolor on paper
7 1/4 x 24 1/2 in. (18.3 x 62.3 cm.)
Signed l.r.: *jl. forain*
c. 1889

The imposing set in the foreground that masks almost half the stage attracts the eye in this work rather than the ballet itself. Concentrated on the lower left, it creates a deliberately exaggerated asymmetry and cuts the composition in two, thereby bringing the scene closer to the spectator. This effect is reinforced by the massive, uniform blackness of the set.

The prominence and position of the stage flat derives directly from compositions Degas developed in his series of fans between 1878 and 1880[1] (*Fan: The Ballet,* fig. no. 33). However, in contrast to Degas, who covers certain fans with gold and silver dust, Forain is not seeking any decorative effect. Instead, he is concentrating on a graphic effect, using only black ink sparingly highlighted with blue wash.

The similarity of technique between this fan and that in *Le Courrier Français*[2] (*Scene at the Opera,* fig. no. 31) indicates that Forain probably intended to reproduce it. The fans resemble each other both in the horizontal lines of the floor and the dancer's spotted tutu.

The scene represents a graceful dancer who appears to be waking up her Prince Charming. This theme cannot easily be attributed to a contemporary ballet, though Forain, perhaps, took inspiration from one of the choreographic interludes frequently included in late nineteenth century operas. Or the scene may derive solely from the artist's imagination.

This fan probably appeared as no. 323 at the Forain exhibition of the Musée des Arts Décoratifs in Paris (1913). At that time, it formed part of the fabulous Impressionist collection assembled by Dr. Viau (1855? - 1939).

Fig. no. 33. Edgar Degas. *Fan: The Ballet,* c. 1879. Watercolor, India ink, silver, and gold on silk. The Metropolitan Museum of Art, New York, bequest of Mrs H.O. Havemeyer, 1929, The H.O. Havemeyer Collection (29.100.554).

Provenance
Georges Viau, Paris; "Succession Georges Viau," Paris, Hotel Drouot, December 11, 1942, no. 23 (entitled *Scène de ballet*); unknown; Galerie Hopkins-Thomas, Paris.

Notes
[1]See Marc Gerstein, "Degas's Fans," *The Art Bulletin,* March 1982, vol. LXIV, no. 1, pp. 105-118.
[2]*Le Courrier Français,* January 20, 1889.

FVF

Cat. no. 40 (Detail)

41.

Dancer with a Rose (fan)
(Danseuse à la rose (éventail))
Watercolor on linen
10 5/8 x 20 in. (27 x 51 cm.)
Dedicated and signed l.l.: *A madame Edwards /
Hommage de / j.l. forain*
c. 1885-1890

In the 1870s and '80s, Japanese fans were very
fashionable in Paris as an element of feminine
attire or wall decorations. This popularity[1] meant
that artists, not only academic painters such as
Gervex and Béraud, but also Impressionists such
as Degas, Pissarro and Gauguin, were called
upon to decorate these fans, like their eighteenth
century predecessors, Lancret and Boucher.

Excited by the experimental range
offered by this new medium, Degas was a
driving force behind the development of this art
form. Fascinated by Japanese art, and fans in
particular, he painted some twenty fans between
1878 and 1880, advising his friends to do likewise. Forain, a young penniless painter, was
always on the look-out for new patrons, and he
soon followed in Degas's footsteps. Thanks to
Degas's influence, Forain presented four fans
and two screen fans at the Fourth "Impressionist" exhibition in 1879.

It seems Forain painted his fans over a
longer period than Degas. The style of *Dancer
with a Rose* appears to belong to the period
1885-90, but it is difficult to date the work since
no detail associates it with any particular ballet.
The off-center position of the dancer at the left
creates an asymmetrical effect[2] reflecting
Degas's influence. The ballerina is standing
before a barely sketched landscape that recalls
Degas's empty spaces.[3]

The fan is dedicated to Mrs. Edwards,
probably the wife of Alfred Edwards (1856-
1914), an art collector and wealthy owner of the
Le Matin newspaper. Edwards had a highly
tumultuous love life, involving several wives and
many mistresses. His last wife was the famous
Misia,[4] a great friend of the Forains. We can
assume that this fan was given to Misia by
Forain before her marriage to Edwards in 1905[5]
and dedicated at a later date. It may, on the
other hand, have been given to Edward's previ-
ous wife between 1885 and 1890.

FVF

Provenance
Offered by the artist to Madame Edwards; unknown; Galerie
Hopkins-Thomas, Paris.

Notes
[1]Marc Gerstein estimated that 2,442,478 fans were imported into
France in 1888 alone (Gerstein, *The Art Bulletin*, p. 107).
[2]See commentary on the *Dancer* (fan), cat. no. 40.
[3]See commentary on the *Dancer in a Colored Tutu* (fan) cat. no.
42.
[4]Misia (1872-1950): see "A Portrait of Jean-Louis Forain" in this
catalogue, note no. 25.
[5]On Misia's marriage to Edwards, see Misia Sert, *Misia*, Paris, 1952,
and Arthur Gold and Robert Fizdale, *Misia-The Life of Misia Sert*,
New York, 1980.

Cat. no. 41 (Detail)

42.

Dancer in a Colored Tutu (fan)

(Danseuse au tutu coloré (éventail))

Black chalk, pastel, gouache on blue paper
12 1/2 x 23 7/8 in. (31.7 x 60.7 cm.)
Signed l.l.: *forain*
c. 1890

Ballet dancing is the most widely used theme on Forain's fans. It is, indeed, the most appropriate subject for this woman's fashion accessory, since dance expresses grace and femininity.

Here, the dancer is sylph-like. Such ethereal figures are found in several of Forain's fans *(Scene at the Opera,* fig. no. 31; *Ballet in the Garden,* cat. no. 39 and *Dancer with a Rose,* cat. no. 41). In his rectangular works Forain tends to depict dancers in the wings or rehearsing, while in this rounded format, he makes them as light as butterflies. Forain may be reflecting Mallarmé's poetic metaphor in which he compares a fan to a wing. Or he could be associating the fan with the illusion of flight that the star ballerinas sought to achieve.[1]

This fan is characterized by empty space. The lower left corner is vacant, and the figure moves before a scarcely suggested setting. Forain is heavily influenced by Degas's style of leaving large areas of his fans uninhabited (*Ballet Girls*, fig. no. 34).

Forain chooses blue paper to represent a moonlit night. The white light falling on the ballerina and the dark shadow projected to her right confirm that this is a nighttime scene. The tutu, decorated with multi-colored spots, adds a note of gayness.

FVF

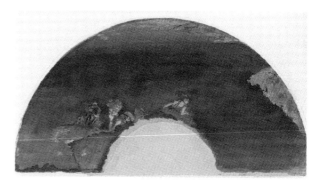

Fig. no. 34. Edgar Degas. *Ballet Girls*, c. 1879. Watercolor, silver and gold on silk. The Metropolitan Museum of Art, New York, bequest of Mrs H.O. Havemeyer, 1929, The H.O. Havemeyer Collection (29.100.555).

Provenance
Noorten, London (1979); Galerie an der Koenigsallee, Düsseldorf (1981); Private collection, The Netherlands; Galerie Hopkins-Thomas, Paris.

Note
[1]This hypothesis was put forward by Marc Gerstein (*The Art Bulletin*, p. 110) for Degas's fans and may also be applicable to those of Forain.

Cat. no. 42 (Detail)

43.

On the Verses of Verlaine, a Rogue Takes a Stroll in the Country

(Sur les vers de Verlaine, promenade du voyou à la campagne)

Pen and India ink and wash on laid rag paper
11 1/8 x 8 5/16 in. (28.3 x 21.1 cm.)
Signed l.r.: *L. Forain*
Inscription l.l.: *Sur des vers de / Verlaine*
m.r.: *Paris je crache pas d'ssus, c'est
rien chouette,
Et comme j'ai une âme de poète,
Tous les dimanches, je quitte ma boête
Et je m'en va avec ma compagne.
A la campagne*

c. 1873

Here, a caricatural suburban couple stands in front of the fortifications which still surrounded Paris at that time. This drawing, still hesitant, is interesting for at least two reasons: it illustrates a verse by Verlaine written in Forain's hand, and because Huysmans describes it in his report on the Fifth "Impressionist" exhibition of 1880 in these terms: "(...) a watercolor notebook, illustrating a poem by Verlaine, is remarkable and sinister. It is called *A Rogue Takes a Stroll in the Country.* A short, stocky man in a long coat, his whiskers sticking out under his tall cap, is strolling along with his lady, an imposing street-walker, with pendulous breasts and protruding stomach which lifts her dress off the ground. The countryside is none other than a public walkway, the view from which is constantly cut off by the city ramparts. It is a visual translation of the writer's fantasy, bringing to reality the ruffian's words quoted in this verse:

> *Paris je crache pas d'ssus, c'est rien chouette,*
> *Et comme j'ai une âme de poète,*
> *Tous les dimanches, je quitte ma boête*
> *Et je m'en va avec ma compagne.*
> *A la campagne*

Mr. Forain has eluded Mr. Verlaine's exaggerated rogue, enlarging the scene and transforming it into a funereal idyll. A shiver runs down one's spine as one examines the gawking posture of these two atrocious beings."[1]

This work, presented at the Fifth "Impressionist" exhibition, thus had its place in the Impressionist adventure. The catalogue includes ten works which are still unidentified due to their extremely succinct titles. *A Rogue Takes a Stroll in the Country* is probably one of the six entries[2] described solely by the word "drawing."

The title given by Huysmans, *A Rogue Takes a Stroll in the Country,* does not correspond to that of Verlaine's poem, which is called "L'Ami de la nature" in the first 1890 edition.[3] A close friend of Verlaine[4] and Rimbaud in the years 1871-73, Forain was familiar with these still unpublished verses.[5]

In his commentary, Huysmans mentions a notebook of watercolors illustrating Verlaine's poem. It is interesting to compare this drawing with the illustration of the second verse which has now been rediscovered (*At the "Guinguette,"* fig. no. 35). This drawing belonged to the writer Boris Kochno (1904-1990).

FVF

Fig. no. 35. J.L. Forain. *At the "Guinguette."* Watercolor, pen and ink. Signed l.l.: *Forain.* Private collection.

Provenance
Boris Kochno Collection, Sotheby's Monaco, October 11, 1991, lot no. 5; Private collection, Monte Carlo; Galerie Hopkins-Thomas, Paris.

Notes
[1] J-K Huysmans, "L'Exposition des Indépendants en 1880," quoted in *L'Art moderne*, Paris, 1986, pp. 112-113.
[2] Nos. 47 to 52, p. 8 of the catalogue of the *Fifth Impressionist Exhibition*, April 1 to 30, 1880, 10, rue des Pyramides, Paris.
[3] "L'Ami de la Nature" was not printed until August 23, 1890 in *Le Chat noir* (*Verlaine, oeuvres poétiques complètes*, Paris, 1962, pp. 127-128 and notes p. 1092).
[4] On Forain's friendship with Verlaine and Rimbaud, see "Reflections on the Life and Art of Jean-Louis Forain" in this catalogue.
[5] This fantasy was composed by Verlaine in 1868.

Paris j'm'en fous d'sur c'est rien
St'homm j'ai un' âm d' [chant]
poète
Tous les Dimanches j'quitt ma boète
Et j'm'en va avec ma com-
pagne
A la campagne

Sur des vers de
Verlaine

J. Forain

44.

A Character in Profile
(Personnage de profil)
Watercolor, pencil on laid rag paper
19 1/8 x 11 1/4 in. (48.7 x 28.7 cm.)
Signed l.r.: *L. Forain*
c. 1876

This watercolor portrays a traveller, probably an Englishman. The scene is most likely in a hotel or café, since the newspaper the man is carrying is attached on its holder, as was the general practice in public places.

Yellow gloves, checkered jacket, round hat, and knotted scarf constitute the accouterments of this grotesque figure. It is characteristic of Forain's first caricatures as the lines still lack confidence, and the silhouette is stiff.

Forain, whose given name was Louis, signs this work L. Forain. He adopted Jean-Louis as a first name in 1880.

FVF

Provenance
Philippe Perrin, Paris; Galerie Hopkins-Thomas, Paris.

45.

The Toff with a Bouquet
(Le Gommeux au bouquet)
Etching on paper 2nd state
15 1/8 x 11 in. (38.4 x 28 cm.)
Signed on plate: *Ls Forain*
Dedicated and signed l.r.: *a Madame de Banville /
respecteusement / L. Forain*
c. 1876

The Toff with a Bouquet is the second etching
printed by Forain. The long, stiff figure of an
opera-patron, wearing evening dress and a top
hat, waits in the wings holding a bouquet in his
hand.

This etching is characteristic of Forain's
early works, in which the artist's originality has
not yet matured. It brings to mind drawings by
Grévin or Somm. Using nervous strokes that lack
density, Forain draws the figure in profile (the
easiest way to render a face). This convenient
solution is also used in *A Character in Profile*
(cat. no. 44). The decor is scant, etched in a
criss-cross pattern.

This is one of Forain's first portrayals of
an opera-goer in the wings, a theme repeated
often throughout his career.[1] This man, typical
of his period, with his fashionable flared trousers, symbolizes the man of the world, rich
enough to be a member of the most select
gentlemen's clubs such as the Jockey, the
Agricole or the Royal. His season ticket to the
opera is above all a pretext for gaining access to
the foyer and the wings, to meet with the dancers. It is, therefore, with a very precise aim in
mind that this clubman prepares to offer his
ballerina this enormous hexagonal bouquet.

This etching is dedicated to Madame de
Banville, the wife of the poet Théodore de
Banville.[2]

FVF

Provenance
Madame Théodore de Banville; Galerie Hopkins-Thomas, Paris; Gift of
Galerie Hopkins-Thomas in honor of John E. Buchanan, Jr.

Notes
[1]The theme of the opera-goer is seen in *Intermission on Stage* (cat. no.
8); *In Front of the Set* (cat. no. 37); *Evening at the Opera* (cat. no. 38);
Dancer at the Bar (cat. no. 52); *Conversation with a Ballerina in the
Wings* (cat. no. 53).
[2]On Théodore de Banville, see commentary on *The Beautiful
Véronique* (cat. no. 6).

References
Alicia Craig Faxon. *Jean-Louis Forain A Catalogue Raisonné of the
Prints*, New York and London, 1982, no. 2.
Marcel Guérin. *J.-L. Forain Aquafortiste*, San Francisco, 1980, no. 2.

46.

Frontispiece Refused for 'Martha'

(Frontispice refusé pour 'Marthe')
Etching with aquatint unequally distributed in the background
12 7/8 x 9 3/4 in. (32.7 x 24.6 cm.)
Unsigned
1879

In 1879, Joris-Karl Huysmans asked his friend Forain to illustrate his Naturalistic novel *Martha*.

Martha is a prostitute; consequently, Forain chooses to portray her in a provocative pose. Her brazen nudity is reinforced by her striped stockings, a typical accouterment of such women (*The Client*, cat. no. 1). Forain handles the paradox with humor, cluttering her with numerous accessories, including umbrella, hat, jewelry, and bows in her braided hair.

Forain was overly daring, and the publisher refused this frontispiece, judging it indecent. He accepted another plate by Forain that depicted a prostitute with empty eyes in an advantageously low-cut dress (fig. no. 36).[1] She insolently holds a bottle as if it were a baby and is backlit by globes of light, a technique often used by Degas.

This engraving has a particular grain, which betrays the influence of Manet. The same is true of the airy, yet concise way Forain handles the etching needle.

This frontispiece evokes the brothel scenes depicted with uncompromising realism by Degas. The dramatic humor of Goya's *Los Caprichos* was conceivably also a source of inspiration.[2] The provocative depiction of Martha's naked body clad in striped stockings is also reminiscent of Rops.

As an ardent partisan of Naturalism, Forain is perfectly in tune with Huysmans' ideas and attracted to the same subjects. "At that time, one could never be Naturalistic enough," said Forain to Marcel Guérin many years later.[3] Huysmans and Forain met in 1876-77 when they were both working with the journal *La République des Lettres*. In 1879, Huysmans was already openly proclaiming his admiration for the young painter[4] and in 1880, asked him to illustrate another work, *Les Croquis parisiens*. The beautiful pastel portrait of Huysmans by Forain[5] dates from this period, during which they "revelled together in Paris."[6]

Many years later, in 1900, their paths crossed again, during a prayer retreat at the Ligugé Abbey. By then, both were devoting their art to their fervent religious faith.

FVF

Fig. no. 36. J.L. Forain. *Frontispiece for Martha*. Etching with aquatint unequally distributed in the background. Signed l.m.: *j.l. forain*. Boston Public Library, Boston, Massachusetts. References: Alicia Craig Faxon. *Jean-Louis Forain A Catalogue Raisonné of the Prints*, New York and London, 1982, no. 15. Marcel Guérin. *J.-L. Forain Aquafortiste*, San Francisco, 1980, no. 14.

Provenance
Gift of Richard Reed Armstrong, Chicago, Illinois.

Notes
[1] Forain illustrated the second edition of *Marthe*, printed in Paris by Dervaux in 1879. The first edition was printed in Belgium.
[2] Goya's etchings, discovered by the young artist at the Cabinet des Dessins of the Musée du Louvre, had been a true revelation for him.
[3] Marcel Guérin, *J.-L. Forain Aquafortiste, Catalogue raisonné*, Paris, 1912, vol. 1, p. 2. In 1910 and 1912, Guérin published the catalogue raisonné of Forain's etchings and lithographs (*J.-L. Forain Lithographe, Catalogue Raisonné*, Paris, 1910; *J.-L. Forain Aquafortiste, Catalogue raisonné*, Paris, 1912). This catalogue was supplemented by Alicia Craig Faxon in 1982 (*Jean-Louis Forain, A Catalogue Raisonné of the Prints*, New York, London).
[4] See J-K Huysmans, "Le Salon de 1879," *L'Art Moderne*, Paris, 1986, p. 85. *L'Art moderne* was first published in 1883.
[5] See fig. no. 24, *Portrait of J-K Huysmans*.
[6] Letter from Huysmans to the Abbé Brousolle, dated January 7, 1901, quoted in Robert Baldick, *La vie de J.-K. Huysmans*, Paris, 1975, p. 97.

References
Alicia Craig Faxon. *Jean-Louis Forain A Catalogue Raisonné of the Prints*, New York and London, 1982, no. 13.
Marcel Guérin. *J.-L. Forain Aquafortiste*, San Francisco, 1980, no. 12.

47.

Portrait of a Seated Man
(Portrait d'homme assis)

Brown crayon on laid paper
12 1/2 x 9 1/4 in. (31.2 x 23.5 cm.)
Signed l.r.: *forain*
Inscription by Forain u.r.: *3.C. de gauche*
c. 1888

This aquiline, bearded profile is handled in the light spirit of the eighteenth century. The man, with drooping hand, who we guess to be seated in an armchair, is of a rare distinction. Early in his career, Forain, like Degas, placed drawing at the pinnacle of Art. With this portrait he achieves a remarkable purity, close to perfection.

This drawing was probably destined for reproduction, since it bears a written inscription by Forain "*3.C. de gauche,*" meaning third column on the left.

FVF

Provenance
Ducousso, Gestas et Bichambre, Pau, France, November 24, 1990;
Galerie Hopkins-Thomas, Paris.

48.

Strolling Couple
(Couple se promenant)

Watercolor on paper
15 7/8 x 12/16 in. (40.2 x 31.2 cm.)
Signed l.r.: *forain*
Oval stamp l.r.: ATELIER / 4307 / J.-L. FORAIN
c. 1890

This couple is contemporary with the drawings delivered by Forain to *Le Courrier Français,* the journal which launched him in his career. From 1887 until 1904, Jean-Louis Forain provided 369 illustrations to *Le Courrier Français,* alongside artists as different as Willette, Heidbrinck, Raffaëlli, Toulouse-Lautrec, and Villon.

    The painter and occasional art critic Jacques-Emile Blanche admired Forain's prodigious memory when he remarked, "The great art and force of Forain is never to draw from life his compositions for *Le Courrier Français.* He constantly makes use of his rare and precious ability to trace from memory the shapes and characters he observes. From time to time, frequently even, he must ask a friend to pose for the fitting or folds of a sleeve, or the position of a hat on the head (...). But after a few brief sketches, his remarkable memory takes over."[1]

FVF

Provenance
Galerie Fisher-Kiener, Paris; Galerie Hopkins-Thomas, Paris.

Note
[1] J.-E. Blanche, "J.-L. Forain," *L'art des deux Mondes,* January 17, 1891, p. 96.

49.

Young Woman with a Veil
(Jeune femme à la voilette)

Black crayon on wove rag paper
12 1/4 x 9 3/8 in. (31.2 x 23.5 cm.)
Signed l.r.: *f*
c. 1890

This powerfully concise sketch illustrates the scope of Forain's drawing. He frequently drew from memory, and this picture is probably no exception.

In a few stokes, without retouching, Forain conjured up the image of a young woman's face and her dreamy expression on the white sheet of paper.

Lost in thought, the young woman with a faraway look, leans on her hand. She appears to be nibbling her finger. With great delicacy, Forain suggests the veil covering her eyes. He highlights the black collar and oversized hat. Remembering that the hat's shadow falls to the right, on her temple, eyebrow and lip, he applies the pencil more darkly in these areas.

By 1890, Forain's personality had matured. His sureness of hand and memory enabled him to develop a concise style. The drawings published in the press no longer have the spindly, caricatural aspect of his earlier works. He adopts a totally personal style which gives a feeling of finality to the least silhouette. "The fluid contours, the stinging lines, the acuity of expression" are admired in 1890 by the famous critic Arsène Alexandre,[1] also an ardent supporter of Toulouse-Lautrec.

Tireless, Forain spent his time drawing and sketching. He did not like to touch up his sketches, preferring to start again on a clean sheet to obtain the exact expression or gesture he desired. Thanks to this method, he achieved the conciseness so characteristic of his art which places him among the greatest draftsmen.

"How long to make this drawing?" "Fifty years," he replied near the end of his life.[2]

FVF

Provenance
Galerie Hopkins-Thomas, Paris.

Notes
[1] Jean Vallery-Radot, *Catalogue Forain* at Bibliothèque Nationale, Paris, 1954, p. 13.
[2] Paul Léon, *Catalogue Forain* at Bibliothèque Nationale, Paris, 1952, p. 6.

50.

Man with a Cane
(L'Homme à la canne)

Black crayon on wove paper
10 13/16 x 7 7/8 in. (27.5 x 20 cm.)
Unsigned
Oval stamp l.r.: ATELIER / 3097 / J.-L. FORAIN
c. 1890-1895

The binocular case slung across this man's coat
indicates that he is at the races, on the day of
the Grand Prix de Paris.

A comparison of this drawing with *A
Character in Profile* (cat. no. 44) brings to light
the level of mastery acquired by Forain after
twenty years of uninterrupted artistic activity.

An intense brutality emanates from this
bourgeois figure, deliberately highlighted by
lines which accentuate the angular contours of
the face, reducing them to a series of triangular
forms: nose, chin, moustache, and ear. These
geometrical shapes are the result of a constant
quest for greater conciseness which leads to a
certain abstraction of the image.

The face is intentionally scored by a
heavy vertical line whose interpretation is
ambiguous. It may represent the chain of the
pince-nez resting on the bridge of his nose, or it
may merely seek to accentuate the effect of
linearity.

FVF

Provenance
Ducousso, Gestas et Bichambre, Pau, France, November 24, 1990;
Galerie Hopkins-Thomas, Paris.

51.

Fashionable Lady with a Hat

(L'Elégante au chapeau)

Blue pencil on laid paper
11 3/16 x 8 1/2 in. (28.3 x 21.6 cm.)
Signed l.r.: *forain*
Oval stamp l.l.: ATELIER / 202 / J.-L. FORAIN
c. 1890

This female figure represents a typical Parisian
lady in her outdoor attire. She is bedecked with
the latest fashion accessories, a boa and hat.

     The drawing is very free, suggesting the
lightness of the boa and the soft material of her
skirt. The face in profile seems to be looking for
someone with whom to converse.

FVF

Provenance
Ducousso, Gestas et Bichambre, Pau, France, November 24, 1990;
Galerie Hopkins-Thomas, Paris.

151

52.

Dancer at the Bar
(Danseuse à la barre)
Watercolor, ink on paper.
10 5/16 x 6 1/2 in. (26.2 x 16.5 cm.)
signed l.r.: *forain*
c. 1885

A ballerina is pursued by her protector all the
way to the rehearsal room. The man leans
confidently on the bar, having invaded the
dancer's private domain.

Rarely has Forain portrayed the opera-
patron with such an invasive attitude. Degas,
who so often depicted dancers at rehearsal,
apparently never portrayed opera-goers at their
side.

FVF

Provenance
Galerie Connaught Brown, London; Galerie Hopkins-Thomas,
Paris.

53.

Conversation with a Ballerina in the Wings

(Conversation avec la ballerine dans les coulisses)

Pen and ink, ink wash on paper mounted on board
13 3/8 x 8 1/2 in. (34 x 21.5 cm.)
Dedicated and signed l.r.: *a Albin Valabrèque /
amicalement / j.l. forain*
c. 1885-1890

Fig. no. 37. Henri de Toulouse-Lautrec. *Divan Japonais,*
poster, 1893. The British Museum, London.

This opera-goer's long white beard emphasizes
the years which separate him from the dancer.
This adventure-seeking old man, dressed up
with a cane and top hat, recalls the silhouette of
the music critic Edmond Dujardin in *Divan
Japonais* (fig. no. 37) by Toulouse-Lautrec.
Following Forain, the young Lautrec also depicts
this type of male predator. However, the situations are different: on Lautrec's poster, the
woman is the star Jane Avril and, as such,
occupies the dominant position. In Forain's
picture, the girl is a young anonymous dancer.
The cane upon which the man is leaning cuts
across the dancer's body, symbolizing male
domination. Some see the canes depicted by
Forain and Lautrec as emblems of the "compul-
sive lechery of the male sex."[1]

The depraved morals condemned by
Forain are also of concern to public opinion, as
shown by this text which appeared in *Le Monde
Parisien,* a journal aimed at a bourgeois reader-
ship interested in social events, and to which
Forain contributed between 1879 and 1881: "(...)
There is no lack of moralists, but how many of
them have the strength to apply their honest
principles? I know some men who would never
dream of eating meat on Good Friday but who,
at midnight on the very same day, do not hesitate to take several bouquets into their carriage,
along with the young flower girl who is selling
them. Before rejecting or casting scorn upon
women, one should provide them with the
means to make an honest living; to pay them
sufficient wages to enable them to eat!

The position of women in our modern
society is such that the most conscientious

working girl is condemned to die of hunger or
throw herself into debauchery."[2]

This drawing is dedicated to Albin
Valabrègue, a journalist at *Le Figaro*. Forain and
Valabrègue worked together on the issue of *Le
Figaro* which came out on January 1, 1885.

FVF

Provenance
Galerie Hopkins-Thomas, Paris.

Notes
[1]Wolfgang Wittrock, *Catalogue complet des estampes de Toulouse-
Lautrec,* 1985, p.27.
[2]Anonymous article dated September 25, 1880.

54.

Dancer

(Danseuse)

Ink wash on paper
15 3/4 x 10 1/4 in. (40 x 26 cm.)
Unsigned
On verso: sketches of four women (ink wash)
c. 1900

In a few pencil strokes, Forain portrays this
resting dancer's diaphanous tutu. Her posture is
languid, and she appears to be dreaming. She
may be wondering if her protector will come
tonight. Or her thoughts may be drifting to the
moment when she rises up the dancing hierar-
chy and becomes a prima ballerina.

FVF

Provenance
Gift of the Forain Family.

55.

My Uncle Gonzague
(Mon oncle Gonzague)

India ink on wove rag paper
13 1/2 x 18 3/4 in. (34.2 x 47.5 cm.)
Signed l.r.: *f*
On verso the inscription: *Mon oncle Gonzague, un beau soir, en rentrant se fit ... recevoir!*
c. 1910

> *My Uncle Gonzague, one fine night*
> *Upon returning home... was in for a fight*

This rhyme is written on the back of the drawing. It is, perhaps, taken from a song of the period which served as inspiration for Forain.

Uncle Gonzague is no beauty, and Forain makes no attempt to transform his features. The artist depicts Mrs. Gonzague with corpulent curves and a menacing eye. We can guess that uncle is returning home sheepishly after a day of pleasure spent with his army companions or his mistress. He tries to make excuses, but there is thunder in the air.

Aware that scenery hinders rather than helps the understanding of a scene, Forain limits the background to empty frames, placing the talking couple in the center of the sheet. He uses wide hatching strokes and gives expressive looks to both faces.

FVF

Provenance
Private collection, Paris; Galerie Hopkins-Thomas, Paris.

Production Notes

Design and Typesetting: Pagemaker 5.0 (Macintosh and Windows)
Fonts: Garamond and Trajan
Color Separations: 175 line screen
Printing: Five Color Heidelberg 28 x 40 Speedmaster
Paper: Cover - Zanders Chromolux 700, cast coated cover, 12 pt.
      Text - International Paper 80 lb. MIRAWEB™ II Recycled Grade
      Contains a Minimum of 10% Deinked Postconsumer Fiber
Binding: "Eurobind" layflat with PUR (Poly Urethane Reactive)
Cover: High Gloss UV Coated